FIGHTING GERMANY'S SPIES

By ***FRENCH STROTHER***

(Originally Published in 1918)

DEDICATED TO

ATTORNEY-GENERAL THOMAS W. GREGORY

Who directed the nation-wide work of arresting and prosecuting German plotters and of interning dangerous enemy aliens.

TABLE OF CONTENTS

FOREWORD

"Fighting Germany's Spies" is published to bring home to the public in a detailed and convincing manner the character of the German activities in the United States. By courtesy of the Bureau of Investigation of the Department of Justice the facts and documents of this narrative have been verified.

INTRODUCTION

Espionage has always been to Americans one of the hateful relics of an outworn political system of Europe from which America was fortunately free. We lived in an atmosphere not tainted with dynastic ambitions or internal oppression. We had no secret agents spying and plotting in other countries and were slow to suspect other countries of doing such things here.

The war, however, disillusioned us. We found our soil to be infested with representatives of an unscrupulous Power which did not hesitate to violate our hospitality and break its most sacred pledges in using this country as a base for unneutral plots against France and Great Britain. We soon learned that these plots were directed against us as well. They were only another manifestation of the spirit which led to the open hostility of Germany which forced us into war.

For a time we were at a great disadvantage in meeting the situation. We had no secret police; we had no laws adequate to deal with these novel offenses.

The Department of Justice met the situation, so far as it could under existing law, by a great enlargement of its Bureau of Investigation, and by the creation of a legal division devoted entirely to problems arising out of the war. Congress substantially supplied the deficiency in the laws by the passage of appropriate statutes. Under the powers obtained in these two directions the Department proceeded vigorously to the suppression of sedition, the internment of enemy aliens, and the prosecution of German agents. Its success is, I feel, attested by the absence of disorder in this country under war-time conditions. Open German activities have long since ceased here and the more subtle operations have been driven so far under cover as to be ineffective. In this work the Department of Justice has had the efficient and loyal aid of private citizens, who have responded generously to a patriotic impulse, through the agency of the American Protective League and similar organizations.

Mr. Strother's narrative covers some of the more outstanding cases of the period when German plotting was at its height. The failure of these plots and the retribution visited upon the evil-doers are evidences, not merely of governmental efficiency, but of that of old, age-old, substantive laws of morality, which Germany as a nation has undertaken to flout—as we now know, in vain—both here and elsewhere.

T. W. GREGORY
Attorney-General.

Washington, D. C.
August 14, 1918.

CHAPTER I

The Inside Story of the Passport Frauds and The First Glimpse of Werner Horn

When Carl Ruroede, the "genius" of the German passport frauds, came suddenly to earth in the hands of agents of the Department of Justice and unbosomed himself to the United States Assistant District Attorney in New York, he said sadly:

"I thought I was going to get an Iron Cross; but what they ought to do is to pin a little tin stove on me."

The cold, strong hand of American justice wrung that very human cry from Ruroede, who was the central figure (though far from the most sinister or the most powerful) in this earliest drama of Germany's bad faith with neutral America—a drama that dealt in forgery, blackmail, and lies that revealed in action the motives of greed and jealousy and ambition, and that ended with three diplomats disgraced, one plotter in the penitentiary, and another sent to a watery grave in the Atlantic by a torpedo from a U-boat of the very country he had tried to serve. This is the story:

Twenty-five days after the Kaiser touched the button which publicly notified the world that Germany at last had decided that "The Day" had come—to be exact, on August 25, 1914—Ambassador Bernstorff wrote a letter effusively addressed to "My very honoured Mr. Von Wedell." (Ruroede had not yet appeared on the scene.) The letter itself was more restrained than the address, but in it Bernstorff condescended to accept tentatively an offer of Wedell's to make a nameless voyage. The voyage was soon made, for on September 24th Wedell left Rotterdam, bearing a letter from the German Consul-General there, asking all German authorities to speed him on his way to Berlin, because he was bearing dispatches to the Foreign Office. Arrived in Berlin, Wedell executed his commission and then called upon his uncle, Count Botho von Wedell, a high functionary of the Foreign Office. He was aflame with a great idea, which he unfolded to his uncle. The idea was approved, and right after the elections in November he was back in New York to put it into execution, incidentally bearing with him some letters handed him by order of Mr. Ballin, head of the Hamburg-American Steamship Company, and another letter "for a young lady who goes to America in the interest of Germany." If unhappy Wedell had let this be his last voyage—but that belongs later in the story.

Wedell's scheme was this: He learned in Berlin that Germany had at home all the common soldiers she expected to need, but that more officers were wanted. He was told that Germany cared not at all whether the 100,000 reservists in America got home or not, but that she cared very much indeed to get the 800 or 1,000 officers in North and South America back to the Fatherland. Nothing but the ocean and the British fleet stood in their way. The ocean might be overcome. But the British fleet——? Wedell proposed the answer: He would buy passports from longshoremen in New York—careless Swedes or Swiss or Spaniards to whom $20 was of infinitely more concern than a mere lie—and send the officers to Europe, armed with these documents, as neutrals travelling on business. Once in Norway or Spain or Italy, to get on into Germany would be easy.

For a few weeks Wedell got along famously. He bought passports and papers showing nativity from Norwegian, Swedish, Danish, and Swiss longshoremen and sailors. Meantime, he got in touch with German reserve officers and passed them on to Europe on these passports.

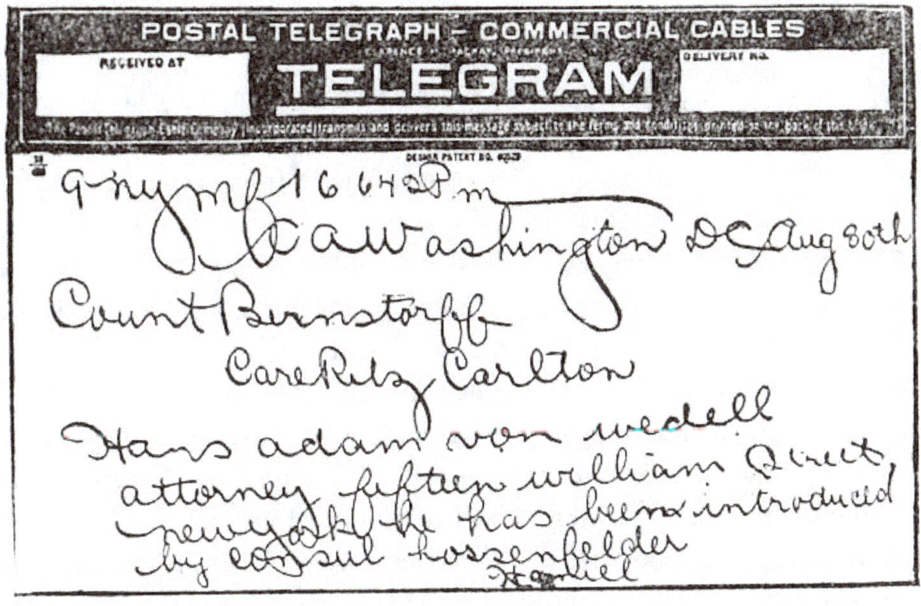

POSTAL TELEGRAPH - COMMERCIAL CABLES

RECEIVED AT

TELEGRAM

DELIVERY NO.

9 ny mf 16 64 P m

C A Washington DC Aug 30th

Count Bernstorff

Care Ritz Carlton

Hans adam von wedell

attorney fifteen william street,

newyork he has been introduced

by consul hossenfelder

Haniel

A GERMAN ATTACHÉ REMINDS BERNSTORFF OF WEDELL

This telegram is from Haniel von Haimhausen, the counsellor of the German Embassy in Washington, and was sent in response to an inquiry from Bernstorff for the name of the man who had offered to act as a messenger to Germany for him. The message reads:

Count Bernstorff, care Ritz Carlton. Hans Adam von Wedell attorney fifteen William Street, New York he has been introduced by consul Hossenfelder, Haniel.

But he was not content with these foreign passports. In the case of a few exceptionally valuable German officers he wished to have credentials that would be above all suspicion. Consequently, he set about to gather a few American passports. Here his troubles began, and here he added the gravest burden to his already great load of culpabilities. For Von Wedell was an

American citizen, and proud of it. But he was prouder still of his German origin and his high German connections, and in his eagerness to serve them he threw overboard his loyalty to the land of his adoption.

Von Wedell applied to a friend of his, a certain Tammany lawyer of pro-German sympathies, who had supplied him with a room belonging to a well-known fraternal organization as a safe base from which to handle his work in passports. What he wanted was an agent who was an American and who had political acquaintanceship that would enable him to work with less suspicion and with wider organization in gathering American passports. Through the lawyer he came in contact with an American, who for the purposes of this story may be called Mr. Carrots, because that is not his name but is remotely like it. Carrots seemed willing to go into the enterprise and at a meeting in Von Wedell's room Von Wedell carefully unfolded the scheme, taking papers from a steel cabinet in the corner to show a further reason why the American passports he already had would soon be useless. This reason was that the Government was about to issue an order requiring that a photograph of the bearer should be affixed to the passport and that on this photograph should appear half of the embossing raised by the impression of the seal of the Department of State. He agreed to pay Carrots $20 apiece for all genuine passports he would supply to him. Carrots accepted his proposal and departed.

Instead of going out to buy passports, he went at once to the Surveyor of the Port of New York, Mr. Thomas E. Rush, and told him what Wedell was doing. Mr. Rush promptly got in touch with his chief in the Treasury Department at Washington, who referred the matter to the State Department, and they, in turn, to the Department of Justice. The result was that Carrots went back to Wedell about a week later and told him he would not be able to go on with the work but would supply someone to take his place. This was satisfactory to Wedell.

In the meantime, Wedell had introduced Carrots to a fellow-conspirator, Carl Ruroede, a clerk in the ship forwarding department of Oelrichs & Company—a man of little position, but fired by the war with the ambition to make a name in German circles that would put him in a position to succeed Oelrichs & Company as the general agent of the North German Lloyd in New York.

About this time Wedell lost his nerve. He was a lawyer and realized some of the possible consequences of certain of his acts. He had had occasion to forge names to two passports; and also he found out that he had reasons to suspect that he was under surveillance. These reasons were very good: he had arranged for the transportation to Italy of a German named Doctor Stark, using the passport of a friend of his in the newspaper business named Charles Raoul Chatillon. Wedell got wind of the fact that Stark had been taken off the steamer *Duca de Aosta* at Gibraltar, and was being detained while the British looked up his credentials.

Wedell by this time was in a most unhappy plight. Bernstorff and Von Papen had no use for him because he had been bragging about the great impression he was going to make upon the Foreign Office in Berlin by his work. If any impressions were to be made upon the Foreign Office in Berlin by anybody in America, Bernstorff and Von Papen wanted to make them. Wedell was so dangerously under suspicion that Von Papen, Von Igel, and his Tammany lawyer friend had all warned him he had better get out of the country. Wedell took their advice and fled to Cuba.

The substitute whom Carrots had promised now entered the case, in the person of a man who called himself Aucher, but who was in reality a special agent of the Department of Justice. Aucher was not introduced to Ruroede, the now active German, and so, when he began his operations, he confronted the very difficult task of making his own connections with a naturally suspicious person.

Carrots had been dealing with Ruroede after Wedell's disappearance; and, by the time he was ready to quit, Ruroede had told him that "everything was off for the present," but that if he would drop around again to his office about January 7, 1915, he might make use of him. Aucher, now on the case, did not wait for that date, but on December 18th called on Ruroede at his office at room 204 of the Maritime Building, at No. 8 Bridge Street, across the way from the Customs House.

In this plainly furnished office Aucher appeared in the guise of a Bowery tough. He succeeded admirably in this rôle—so well, indeed, that Ruroede afterward declared that he "succeeded wonderfully in impressing upon my mind that he was a gangman, and I had visions of slung shots, pistol shots, and holdups" when he saw him. Aucher opened the conversation by announcing:

"I'm a friend of Carrots."

"That's interesting," was Ruroede's only acknowledgment.

"He's the guy that's getting them passports for you," went on Aucher, "and all I wants to know is, did you give him any cush?"

"What do you mean?" asked Ruroede.

"Nix on that!" Aucher exclaimed. "You know what I mean. Did you give that fellow any money?"

To which Ruroede replied: "I don't see why I should tell you if I did."

"Well," retorted Aucher, "I'll tell you why. I'm the guy that delivers the goods, and he swears he never got a penny from you. Now did he?"

It was at this point that Ruroede had his visions of slung shots, so he admitted he had paid Carrots $100 only a few days before.

"Well," demanded Aucher, "ain't there going to be any more?"

"Nope. Not now," Ruroede replied. "Maybe next month."

"Now see here," said Aucher. "Let's cut this guy out. He's just nothing but a booze fighter, and he's been kidding you for money without delivering the goods. What's the matter with just fixing it up between ourselves?"

Ruroede now tried to put Aucher off till Christmas, having recalled meanwhile that the steamer *Bergensfjord* was to sail on January 2d, and that he might need passports for officers travelling on that ship. But Aucher protested that he was "broke," and further impressed on Ruroede that he had gotten no money from Carrots or Wedell for his work for them. He also produced six letters written by the State Department in answer to applicants for passports, and finally convinced Ruroede of his good faith and that he ought to start him to work right away. They haggled over the price, and finally agreed on $20 apiece for passports for native-born Americans and $30 apiece for passports of naturalized citizens—the higher price for getting the latter because they involved more red-tape and hence more risk. Aucher was to come back on December 24th and bring the passports and get some money on account.

On that day Aucher called at Ruroede's office, and after further quarrelling about Carrots and his honesty, Ruroede declared that he was ready to do business. Aucher objected to the presence of a young man in the room with them, and Ruroede replied:

"Oh, he's all right. He's my son, and you needn't be afraid to talk with him around."

Aucher then produced an American passport, No. 45,573, made out in the name of Howard Paul Wright, for use in Holland and Germany. It was a perfectly good passport, too, as it had been especially made out for the purpose by the Department of State at the request of the Department of Justice. It bore Mr. Bryan's genuine signature, and a photograph of "Wright," who was another agent of the Bureau of Investigation. Aucher also declared he was on the way toward getting the other five passports. Ruroede threw the Wright passport on his desk and said:

"I'll keep this. Go ahead and get the others."

"What about money?" demanded Aucher.

"I'll pay you $25 for it—no, I'll do better than that. To show you I mean business, take that," and he threw a $100 bill on the table. Ruroede also gave Aucher photographs of four German officers, and begged him to get passports right away to fit their descriptions, because he wanted to get these men off on the Norwegian Line steamer *Bergensfjord*, sailing January 2d. He added that the officers of the Norwegian Line had all been "smeared" (otherwise "fixed") and that they would "stand for anything." He also said that he would take at least forty more passports from Aucher, and that he would want them right along for six months or a year, depending on the length of the war.

Aucher delivered two more passports to Ruroede in his office on the morning of December 30th. Ruroede was rather indifferent about getting them, because—alas for the glory of the "invincible" Prussian arms!—two of his German officers had gotten "cold feet" and had refused to go. Ruroede told Aucher to come back at two o'clock and he would give him $100. Aucher invited Ruroede to have luncheon with him, and as they left the building Ruroede explained with much pride that he had chosen his office here because the building had several entrances on different sides of the block, and he used one entrance only a few days at a time and then changed to another to avoid suspicion.

The Government's special agent complimented him highly on this bit of cleverness in the art of evasion. Five minutes later the two were sitting at a lunch counter with another special agent casually lounging in and taking the seat next to his fellow operative, where he could overhear and corroborate the account of Ruroede's conversation.

After a discussion of Wedell's forgeries and present whereabouts, and a further discussion of the buying of passports (in which Ruroede confided to Aucher that "there is a German fund that was sent over here for that purpose") the pair walked back toward Ruroede's office. At the Whitehall Street entrance Ruroede told Aucher to come around to the Bridge Street entrance in about fifteen minutes to get the money, and that in the meantime he would send his son out to cash a check so that he could deliver it in bills. Aucher spent part of the fifteen minutes signalling to four other special agents who had reinforced him, and then went around to the Bridge Street entrance, with one of his confederates in sight.

In a few moments, Ruroede's son rushed out with a bank book in his hand. Aucher stopped him and told him he ought to have a coat on, a device to let Aucher's fellow operative see him talking to the boy so he could identify him. The boy then went on to the bank, followed by Aucher's confederate, who saw him cash the check and followed him back to the building.

When the boy returned, Aucher again spoke to him and said: "Tell your father I will be in the café at Whitehall and Bridge streets and that he is to meet me there. I don't think it is a good thing for anybody to see me hanging around the front entrance."

Aucher then went on into the café and signalled to the other three operatives to follow him. He took a seat in a bootblack's chair near the entrance and proceeded to have his shoes blacked. In about ten minutes Ruroede's son came out and was about to pass by him when Aucher hailed him. Ruroede's son then took a sealed envelope from his inside pocket and handed it to Aucher.

"Where is your father?" Aucher asked.

"Oh, he's got a man upstairs with him," said young Ruroede, "and he couldn't come down."

"Wait a minute," said Aucher, and tore open the envelope in the presence of Ruroede's son, and, so that the other special agents could see him do it, counted out ten $10 bills, $100 in all. As he was counting them, the operative who had followed Ruroede's son to the bank came in and shouldered the boy to one side and then stood right by him while the money was being counted. Aucher went on to impress on Ruroede's son that business was business and that the best of friends sometimes fell out over money matters; that his father might have unintentionally counted out $80 or $90 instead of the full $100 and it was safer to take some precautions than to take a chance of creating bad blood between them. He then invited Ruroede's son to have a drink with him, which he did, both of them taking the strongest Prussian drink—milk. When they were about to part on Whitehall Street Aucher told Ruroede's son to tell his father he would be down the next morning with the other two passports he had mentioned to him, and again impressed on the boy the importance of accuracy in money matters. Aucher then returned to headquarters with the other special agents and listed the distinguishing marks on the bills and marked them for future identification.

GERMAN AGENTS WHO DEALT IN FRAUDULENT PASSPORTS

H. A. Von Wedell Carl Ruroede

AMERICANS HIRED TO BLOW UP SHIPS AND FACTORIES

C. C. Crowley Lewis J. Smith

The next morning Aucher telephoned to Ruroede and told him he had been able to get only one of the two passports he wanted, giving as the excuse for his failure to get the other the story that it had been promised to him by a man working on a job in Long Island and that this man had met with an accident and was in the hospital; that it would take a day or two to go out there to get a written order from him to a brother who would turn the passport over to Aucher. Ruroede accepted an invitation to take luncheon with Aucher at Davidson's restaurant at the corner of Broad and Bridge streets.

An English translation of the letter, the first and last pages of which are shown above, follows:

S. S. Kristianiafjord, Bordjen, Nov. 20, 1914. Most honoured Mr. Ruroede: As you see, my voyage across succeeded magnificently with your kind help. The weather until Sunday was fine—then three days' storm. The beginning was not of a nature to inspire confidence, for five hours after we had left New York we were stopped by a cruiser and for two hours the ship's papers were searched for contraband. We had also some copper on board, but that was for Norway, whereupon they let us go. Our Captain then ran straight North to the 63 latitude. We nearly touched Iceland in order to get out of the way of other cruisers. It was only while we were making for Bergen from a northerly direction yesterday that a cruiser overtook and stopped us, and for a short while six of your men were feeling pretty shaky, especially I, for among the 18 first-class passengers, more than half were Germans, also a former vice-consul from Japan (now captain of cavalry) of the Bonn Hussars, Naval Officer from China, and others. The incident lasted only a half hour. After searching for ship's papers, the gentlemen disappeared, and we breathed more freely, and drank a cocktail to the —— and your prosperity. Once more many thanks for your assistance. May you help many others as well. With best wishes, Yours, Edward Eaton, in Japan named Eichelbert.

Shortly after noon they met on the street and went into the restaurant together. A few minutes after they were seated two of the special agents came in and took a table about fifteen feet away. After Aucher had ordered lunch for himself and Ruroede, he took out of his pocket another of the series of genuine passports supplied by the State Department, to which he had attached one of the photographs Ruroede had given him for this purpose. He handed the passport to Ruroede, who opened only one end of it, just enough to glance at the photograph and seal.

"That's fine," said Ruroede, and was about to slip it into his pocket when Aucher seized it and exclaimed:

"Fine? I should say," and opened the passport wide so that one of the other special agents could see the red seal on it. "Just look at that description. Eh? He is the fellow with the military bearing and I gave him a description I figured a man like him should answer to."

At this point, the special agent who had seen the seal left his seat at the table and walked to the cashier's desk. As he passed, Ruroede was holding the passport in his hands and Aucher was pointing out the description. Ruroede then put the passport into his pocket and said again: "That's fine."

Aucher then opened a discussion of Von Wedell's career and disappearance. Ruroede was very contemptuous of the missing man. "He was a plain fool," he said. "He paid $3,500 altogether and got very little in return. A fellow came to him one day and told him he could get him American passports and Von Wedell said: 'All right; go ahead.' The fellow returned later and said he would have to have some expense money and he gave him $10. A little while later a friend of the first man came to Von Wedell wanting expense money. When Von Wedell decided to put him off, he became threatening and Von Wedell, fearing he might tell the Government authorities, gave *him* some money. A few days later about twenty fellows came looking for Von Wedell. But quite aside from that sort of business Von Wedell's foolishness in forging names on two American passports is the thing that made him get away."

"Did I understand you to say," asked Aucher, "that he had gone to join his wife?"

"No," replied Ruroede, "she will be in Germany before him. She sailed last Tuesday. He went to Cuba first and there got a Mexican passport of some sort that will take him to Spain. He ought to be in Barcelona to-day and from there go to Italy, and then from there work his way into Germany."

"You say Von Wedell spent $3,500 of his own money?" Aucher asked.

"No, no," exclaimed Ruroede, "he got it from the fund."

"Well, who puts up this money—who's back of it?"

"The Government."

"The German Government?"

"Yes," said Ruroede. "You see it is this way: There is a captain here who is attached to the German Embassy at Washington. He has a list of German reservists in this country and is in touch with the German consulates all through the country and in Peru, Mexico, Chile, etc. He gets in touch with them, and the consuls send reservists, who want to go to the front, on to New York. When they get here, this captain tells them: 'Well, I can't do anything for you, but you go down to see Ruroede.' Sometimes he gives them his personal card."

"Is this captain in reserve?" Aucher interrupted.

"Oh, no, he is active," Ruroede replied. "You see," he continued, "he draws on this fund for $200 or $300 or $1,000, whatever he may need, and the checks are made to read 'on account of reservists.' You see, they have to have food and clothing, also, so there is nothing to show that this money is paid out for passports or anything like that. I meet this captain once a week or so, and tell him what I am doing and he gives me whatever money I need. You see, there must be no connection between him and me; no letters, no accounts, nothing in writing. If I were caught and were to say what I have told you, this captain would swear that he never met me in his life before."

Who this captain was became perfectly clear through an odd happening two days later. On that day, January 2, 1915, Aucher telephoned to Ruroede at his office and made an appointment to meet him at a quarter of one. This meeting will doubtless remain forever memorable in Ruroede's experience.

At twelve-thirty a whole flock of special agents left the office of the Bureau of Investigation of the Department of Justice in the Park Row Building. There were nine representatives of the Department in the group. When they got near Ruroede's office they were joined by two others who had been shadowing Ruroede. They had located him at the Eastern Hotel, several blocks away, where he was at the moment with one of the German officers who planned to sail that day on the Norwegian Line steamer *Bergensfjord* with one of the false passports.

Shortly after one o'clock one of the special agents notified the group that Ruroede had returned to his office and then this operative, and one other, went to the Customs House and stationed themselves at a window opposite

Ruroede's office to wait for a signal which Aucher was to give when he had delivered the passport to Ruroede.

When Aucher met Ruroede in the latter's office Ruroede's son was present, but in a few moments the younger man took his leave, and his departure was noted by one of the agents outside. After a few minutes' conversation Aucher handed Ruroede the missing passport and made his signal to the two men inside the Customs House window. These men reported to the main group on the street and thereupon the whole flock descended on Ruroede's office and placed both Ruroede and Aucher under arrest.

They seized all of Ruroede's papers before they took him away, including the passport which Aucher had just delivered to him. Aucher put up a fight against his brother officers, so as to make Ruroede believe that his arrest was genuine, but was quickly subdued and taken away. A few minutes later Ruroede also was taken from his office over to the offices of the Bureau of Investigation, but to another room than Aucher. Operatives were left behind in Ruroede's office, and in a little while Ruroede's son came in. He, too, was arrested and taken to still another part of the office of the Bureau.

Now there entered Ruroede's office a stranger, who to this day does not know that he unwittingly gave the officers of the United States Government the information that Captain Von Papen was directly responsible for the passport frauds. This man entered while one of the operatives was busily gathering up the papers on Ruroede's desk. He said he wanted to see Mr. Ruroede. The operative asked him what his business was, and he replied that he had a letter to give him; and answering an inquiry, he said this letter was given him by Captain Von Papen, to be delivered to Ruroede.

The operative calmly informed the caller that he was Mr. Ruroede's son and that he could give the letter to him. The stranger refused, so the operative told him that his "father," Ruroede, would be in in a few minutes. After the few minutes were up, he told the caller that he was sure that his "father" would not return after all, and that he had better go with him to where his "father" was. The stranger agreed and they left the office together, the operative taking him directly to the office of the Bureau of Investigation.

On the way, the stranger decided to give him the letter from Captain Von Papen, and also told him that he had come from Tokyo by way of San Francisco; that he was very anxious to get back to Germany; and that he was sorry he was not sailing on the boat leaving that day. He knew, he said, that Ruroede had a great many officers sailing on the ship that day, and asked if he thought the operative's "father" could make an arrangement to start him to Germany, too. He gave as a reason for his urgency the fact that he had with him eight trunks which contained very important papers in connection with the war that should be delivered in Berlin without delay.

Upon arriving at the office of the Bureau of Investigation the operative excused himself for a moment and went into another room, where he concocted a plan with a fellow agent to pose as the senior Ruroede. The operative then brought the stranger in and introduced his confederate as his father. The stranger gave this agent of the Department his card which was printed in German and, which translated into English, read, "Wolfram von Knorr, Captain of Cruiser, Naval Attaché, Imperial German Embassy, Tokyo."

But let us leave the guileless caller in the hands of the guileful agent of Justice for a few moments, returning to him a little later.

Meanwhile, four of the agents from the Department—the minute they received the signal that Ruroede was under arrest—hastened to the Barge Office dock and boarded the revenue cutter *Manhattan*, on which they overtook the Norwegian Line steamship *Bergensfjord* at four o'clock, about one half hour after it had set sail. They were accompanied by several customs inspectors and ordered the *Bergensfjord* to heave to. All the male passengers on board were lined up. Strange as it may seem, they discovered four Germans, of such unmistakable names as Sachse, Meyer, Wegener, and Muller, travelling under such palpably English and Norwegian names as Wright, Hansen, Martin, and Wilson. Stranger still, they all turned out to be reserve officers in the German army. Sache proved to be travelling as none other than our friend "Howard Paul Wright," for whom Aucher had supplied Ruroede with the passport—as, indeed, he had for the three others.

Meanwhile, Ruroede was the centre of another little drama that lasted until well toward midnight. He was being urged by the United States Assistant District Attorney to "come across" with the facts about his activities in the passport frauds, and he had stood up pretty well against the persuasions and hints of the attorney and the doubts and fears of his own mind. About eleven o'clock at night, as he was for the many'th time protesting his ignorance and his innocence, another agent of the Bureau of Investigation walked across the far end of the dimly lit room—in one door and out another—accompanied by a fair-haired lad of nineteen.

"My God!" exclaimed Ruroede, "have they got my son, too? The boy knows nothing at all about this."

This little ghost-walking scene, borrowed from "Hamlet," broke down Ruroede's reserve, and he came out with pretty much all the story, ending the melancholy exclamation with which this story began: "I thought I was going to get an Iron Cross; but what they ought to do is to pin a little tin stove on me."

Ruroede admitted that he had met Captain Von Papen in New York frequently and that Von Papen had given him money at different times, but he denied that this money was given him for use in furnishing passports. On this point he stood fast, and to this day he has not directly implicated Von Papen in these frauds, though it cost him a sentence of three years in the Federal penitentiary at Atlanta, imposed just two months later.

One thing Ruroede did confess, however, and in doing so he was the Hand of Fate for the timorous Von Wedell. Ruroede confessed that his assertion to Aucher, that Wedell was then in Barcelona, was a lie, and that the truth was that Wedell had recently returned from Cuba and was aboard the *Bergensfjord*! This confession came too late to serve that day, for the agents of the Bureau had by that time left the ship with their four prisoners and the *Bergensfjord* was out to sea. But Fate had nevertheless played

Wedell a harsh trick, for the processes of extradition were instantly put in motion with what strange results will in a few moments be made clear.

FORMERLY BARDIN'S

TELEPHONES 103 / 104

HOTEL ST. GEORGE
FELIX FIEGER, PROPRIETOR
NYACK-ON-HUDSON

26. Dez. 1914

Seiner Exzellenz
dem Kaiserlich Deutschen Botschafter
Herrn Grafen von Bernstorff
Washington, D.C.

Euer Exzellenz
erlaube ich mir ganz gehorsamst die folgenden Thatsachen zu unterbreiten:
Es scheint, dass der Versuch gemacht wurde, bei Ihnen den Eindruck hervorzurufen, dass ich meinen Posten in New York vorzeitig verliess. Das ist nicht wahr:
Meine Arbeit war gethan. Ich liess bei meiner Abreise den Dienst durchorganisiert und bis in das kleinste Detail ausgearbeitet in den Händen meines von mir ausgesuchten Nachfolgers, Herrn Carl Ruroede, zurück und blieb, trotz vielfacher Warnungen noch 8 Tage lang in New York, um ihm die nötigen letzten Anweisungen zu geben und um die mir von deutschen Offizieren auf das [illegible] gebetenen Expressen bis zur Durchfahrt [?] [illegible] durch Gibraltar im Zaume zu halten, was mir gelang. Herr Ruroede wird Ihnen bestätigen, dass er dann meine umfassenden Vorarbeiten, bei denen ich keinen ordentlichen Wege [illegible] und bei denen ich

t gewesen. Und ich fahre jetzt mit dem Bewusstsein nach Deutschland zurück, meine Pflicht so gut ich es verstand, gethan und meine Aufgabe erfüllt zu haben.

Euer Excellenz aber danke ich für alle bisher bewiesene Liebenswürdigkeit und namentlich für die Aufnahme, die Sie meiner Frau bereiteten, die leider, sehr gegen meinen Willen, jetzt aus Deutschland hierher zurückkehrte.

Mit dem Ausdruck der vorzüglichsten Hochachtung bin ich Euer Excellenz

ganz ergebenster

Hans Adam von Wedell.

VON PAPEN AND ALBERT APPEAR AS UNNEUTRAL PLOTTERS

This letter [of which the facsimiles are of the first and last pages] was written by Wedell to Bernstorff to justify his action in abandoning the work of gathering passports for fraudulent use. The full text follows, in English. It is an interesting document, not only because it reveals a lot of weak human nature in the agents of "German efficiency" but also because it definitely revealed Von Papen and Albert as principals in the German plots as early as three months after the war started:

HOTEL ST. GEORGE Felix Fieger, Proprietor, Nyack-on-Hudson, December 26, 1914. His Excellency The Imperial German Ambassador, Count Von Bernstorff, Washington, D. C. Your Excellency: Allow me most obediently to put before you the following facts: It seems that an attempt has been made to produce the impression upon you that I prematurely abandoned my post in New York. That is not true.

I. My work was done. At my departure I left the service well organized and worked out to its minutest details, in the hands of my successor, Mr. Carl Ruroede, picked out by myself, and, despite many warnings, still tarried for several days in New York in order to give him the necessary final directions and in order to hold in check the blackmailers thrown on my hands by the German officers until after the passage of my travellers through Gibraltar; in which I succeeded. Mr. Ruroede will testify to you that without my suitable preliminary labors, in which I left no conceivable means untried and in which I took not the slightest consideration of my personal weal or woe, it would be impossible for him, as well as for Mr. Von Papen, to forward officers and "aspirants" in any number whatever, to Europe. This merit I lay claim to and the occurrences of the last days have unfortunately compelled me, out of sheer self-respect, to emphasize this to your Excellency.

II. The motives which induced me to leave New York and which, to my astonishment, were not communicated to you, are the following:

1. I knew that the State Department had, for three weeks, withheld a passport application forged by me. Why?

2. Ten days before my departure I learnt from a telegram sent me by Mr. Von Papen, which stirred me up very much, and further through the omission of a cable, that Dr. Stark had fallen into the hands of the English. That gentleman's forged papers were liable to come back any day and could, owing chiefly to his lack of caution, easily be traced back to me.

3. Officers and aspirants of the class which I had to forward over, namely the people, saddled me with a lot of criminals and blackmailers, whose eventual revelations were liable to bring about any day the explosion of the bomb.

4. Mr. Von Papen had repeatedly urgently ordered me to hide myself.

5. Mr. Igel had told me I was taking the matter altogether too lightly and ought to—for God's sake—disappear.

6. My counsel, ... had advised me to hastily quit New York, inasmuch as a local detective agency was ordered to go after the passport forgeries.

7. It had become clear to me that eventual arrest might yet injure the worthy undertakings and that my disappearance would probably put a stop to all investigation in this direction.

How urgent it was for me to go away is shown by the fact that, two days after my departure, detectives, who had followed up my telephone calls, hunted up my wife's harmless and unsuspecting cousin in Brooklyn, and subjected her to an interrogatory.

Mr. Von Papen and Mr. Albert have told my wife that I forced myself forward to do this work. That is not true. When I, in Berlin, for the first time heard of this commission, I objected to going and represented to the gentleman that my entire livelihood which I had created for myself in America by six years of labor was at stake therein. I have no other means, and although Mr. Albert told my wife my practice was not worth talking about, it sufficed, nevertheless, to decently support myself and wife and to build my future on. I have finally, at the suasion of Count Wedell, undertaken it, ready to sacrifice my future and that of my wife. I have, in order to reach my goal, despite infinite difficulties, destroyed everything that I built up here for myself and my wife. I have perhaps sometimes been awkward, but always full of good will and I now travel back to Germany with the consciousness of having done my duty as well as I understood it, and of having accomplished my task.

With expressions of the most exquisite consideration, I am, your Excellency.

Very respectfully,
(Signed) HANS ADAM VON WEDELL.

Now we may appropriately return to the conference between the guileless stranger from Tokyo and the guileful agent of the Bureau of Investigation, in another room. The guileless stranger from Tokyo revealed what Ruroede would not disclose—and revealed it all unconsciously. He talked so frankly with "young Ruroede's father" that he told several most important things. For one, Captain Von Knorr declared that Captain Von Papen had sent him. Whereupon the pretended Ruroede asked him whether the fact that he was expected to assist Von Knorr back to Europe was known to the German Embassy at Washington. To this Von Knorr replied:

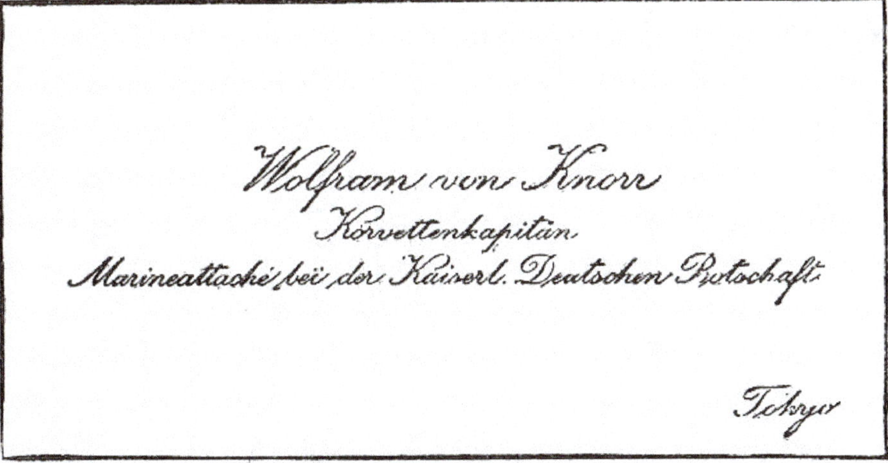

THE CARD OF "THE GUILELESS STRANGER FROM TOKYO"

“Of course. I just had a talk with Captain Von Papen right here in New York.”

“Ruroede” still insisted on having better proof that Von Knorr came directly from the Embassy, to which Von Knorr retorted that “Von Papen has had sufficient dealings with you for you to know that any one sent by him to you is all right.”

Finding himself dealing with a somewhat reluctant saviour, Von Knorr adopted a conciliatory mood and slapped his broad hand several times on “Ruroede’s” left breast, saying: “That chest ought to have something”—meaning a decoration from Berlin.

After some verbal sparring, Von Knorr was allowed to drift off the scene as innocently as he had entered it, and he has yet to learn that his visit was in an office of American law and that his dealings were with the officers of Justice.

But he left behind a legacy quite as valuable as his carefully remembered spoken words. This legacy was the paper which he had brought from Franz von Papen. This paper proved to be not a letter, but rather a typewritten memorandum—though all doubt as to its origin was removed by the innocent insistence of Von Knorr that he had come with it from Von Papen’s hand.

THE OFFICIAL GERMAN PLOTTERS AT WASHINGTON

Above, Ambassador Count Johann von Bernstorff; left, Capt. Franz von Papen, Military Attaché; right, Capt. Karl Boy-Ed, Naval Attaché

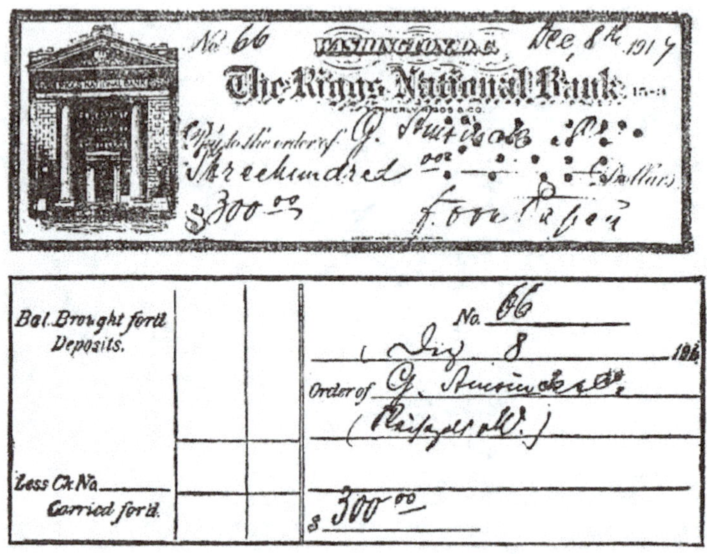

No. 66

The Riggs National Bank

$300.00

Bal. Brought forw'd

Deposits.

Less Ck. No.

Carried forw'd.

No. 66

Order of

$ 300.00

VON PAPEN BECOMES ACCESSORY TO A CRIME

Though this check was made out in favor of G. Amsinck & Co., the German-American bankers of New York, the counterfoil bears the notation "Traveling expense v W," that is, "von Wedell." This check was sent him by Von Papen to enable him to escape after he had forged signatures to two fraudulent passports and realized that he was under surveillance—Von Papen thus becoming accessory after the fact to a crime against American laws.

Two most important facts emerged ultimately from a study of this innocent bit of paper. When Ruroede was arrested, among other papers taken from his desk by the officers of the law were numerous typewritten sheets containing lists of names of German officers, their rank, and other facts about them. Ruroede never would admit that these were from Von Papen, but that admission was made for him by a far more trustworthy testimony than his own. This testimony was an expert comparison, under a powerful magnifying glass of the typewriting on these sheets and the typewriting on the Von Knorr memorandum which had undoubtedly come from Von Papen. They were beyond all questioning identical. The same typewriter had written all. By this little microscopic test Von Papen and the other ruthless underlings of Germany were first brought tangibly within sight of their ultimate expulsion from this country, for crimes of which the passport frauds were the least odious.

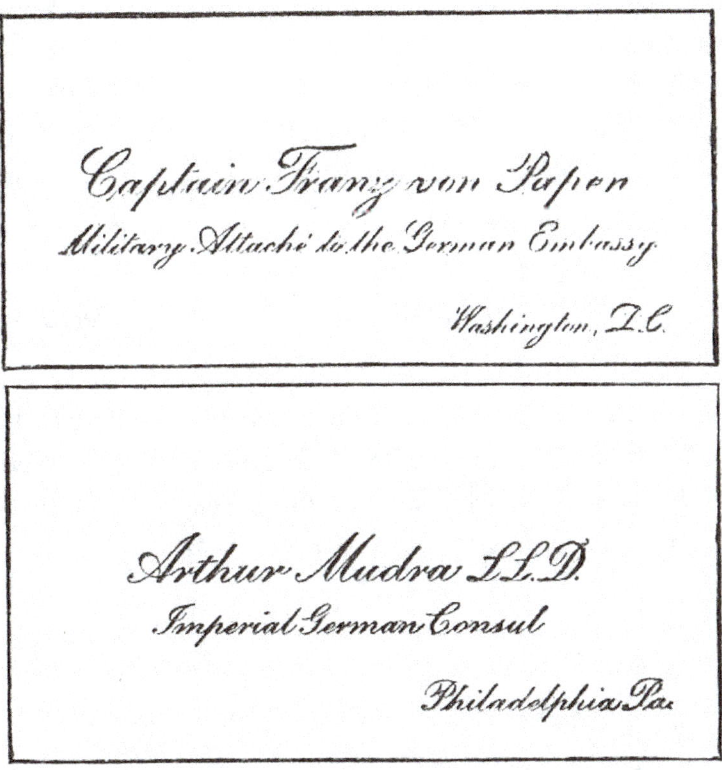

TWO OF RUROEDE'S VISITORS' CREDENTIALS

These cards were presented by two German officers in search of fraudulent passports. They were sent by Von Papen and Mudra (German Consul at Philadelphia), who both frequently directed such officers to Ruroede for this purpose.

The other pregnant fact about the Von Knorr memorandum was that the eyes of Justice rested on the name of *Werner Horn* and lingered long enough to fix that name in memory. Here first swam into its ken the man who tried to destroy the international bridge at Vanceboro, Maine, and whose story is one of the most romantic and adventurous of all the German plotters!

One last touch in this drama: A few moments ago we left Von Wedell—ambitious, timorous Von Wedell—on the high seas bound for Norway. But Fate was after him. Ruroede's moment of weakness—his moment of pique, when he swore he would not shoulder all this bitterness alone—had set her on his trail. A cable message to London, a wireless from the Admiralty, and then—this entry in the logbook of the *Bergensfjord* for Monday, January 11, 1915:

All male first and second class passengers were gathered in the first-class dining saloon and their nationality inquired into.

About noon, the boarding officer of the Cruiser —— (English) went back and reported to his ship. About 0:45 P. M. *he came over with orders again to take off six German stowaways and two suspected passengers. These passengers were according to ship's berth list as follows:*

1. Rosato Sprio, Mexican, Destination Bergen, Cabin 71, second-class....

Rosato Sprio admitted after close examination to be H. A. Wedell. Claimed to be a citizen of the United States....

Dr. Rasmus Bjornstad claimed to be a Norwegian....

As both passengers apparently were travelling under false pretense, the Captain did not feel justified to protest against the detention of the two passengers. These were accordingly ... taken off and put on board the Auxiliary Cruiser ——.

Unhappy Wedell! "The Cruiser ——" was a ship that never made port. Wedell's high connections in the German Foreign Office could not save him from the activities of the high officials of the German Admiralty. A U-boat fired a torpedo into "the Cruiser ——" and sent her to the bottom with Rosato Sprio, *alias* H. A. Wedell, aboard.

Exeunt Wedell and Ruroede.

Enter Werner Horn.

CHAPTER II

The Inside Story of Werner Horn and The First Glimpse of the Ship Bombs

The real mystery in the case of Werner Horn is this: Who was the man in Lower 3? (If he had only known——!) Because, except for this one missing fact, the story of Werner Horn is as clear as day. It is the story of a brave man, too honest to lie with a straight face, who was used by the villainous Von Bernstorff and Von Papen only after they had lied without a quiver, on at least three vital points, to him. He meant to fight the enemy of his country as a soldier fights, and they cynically sent him on an errand which they meant should be an errand of miscellaneous crime, including murder. He was to go to a felon's death for this one of the many devilish plots they were concocting against American lives, while they lived in luxury in Washington and lied with smiling faces to the representatives of the people whose hospitality they were betraying. There have been few more despicably outrageous, more cold-blooded crimes than this—except that other one (also of their devising) in the ship bombs case; but that is another story, to be told later.

The story of Werner Horn begins in Guatemala. Horn was the manager of a coffee plantation at Moka. He had seen ten years of service in the German Army when, in 1909, he got a furlough from the authorities in Cologne permitting him to go to Central America for two years. This furlough writes him down as an "Oberleutnant on inactive service." That means, roughly, that he was a first lieutenant of the German Army, out of uniform but subject to call ahead of all other classes of men liable for military duty. Then came the war.

Two hours after word of "The Day" reached Moka, Werner Horn was packed and on his way to Germany. From Belize he sailed to Galveston, where he spent two weeks looking in vain for passage. Then on to New York, where he tried for a month to sail. Finding that impossible, he went to Mexico City and there learned that another man in Guatemala had his job. He had just found another one, on an American coffee plantation at Salto de Aguas, in Chiapas, and was about to go there by launch from Frontera, when he got a card telling him to try again to get to Germany. By

December 26th he was back in New Orleans, and a few days later he was lodging in the Arietta Hotel on Staten Island.

Now began a series of conferences with Von Papen. Horn was afire with honest zeal to serve the Fatherland, and Von Papen was unscrupulous as to how he did it. When he could not get passage for him back to Germany, Von Papen determined to use this blond giant (Horn is six feet two) for another purpose. He then unpacked his kit of lies.

A little after the midnight of Saturday, December 29, 1914, a big German in rough clothes and cloth cap entered the Grand Central Station carrying a cheap brown suitcase. A porter seized it from him with an expansive smile. The smile faded long before they reached Car 34 of the one o'clock New Haven train to Boston. "Boss, yoh sho' has got a load o' lead in theah," was his puffing comment as he got his tip. The German grinned, and a few minutes later swung the suitcase carelessly against the steam-pipes under Lower 3, and clambered to the upper. A suitcase full of dynamite—and the man in Lower 3 slept on.

Several people on the Maine Central train that left North Station, Boston, at eight o'clock the next morning, afterward identified the big blond German who left it at Vanceboro, Maine, at six forty-five that evening. None of them recalled his baggage.

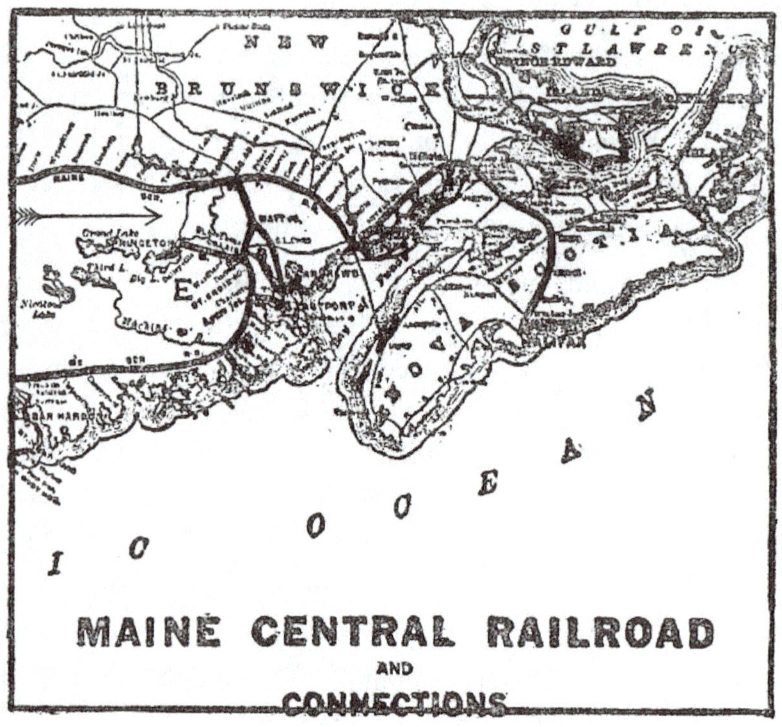

WERNER HORN'S PLAN OF ESCAPE

The pencilled line left from Vanceboro and down to Princeton was Horn's own mark upon the map of the route by which he hoped to escape after he had blown up the international bridge. He did not know the country and hence did not calculate upon the wilderness he was planning to traverse, unguided, in the dead of a New England winter. The pencilled ring around St. John, N. B., gives the cue to his purpose in blowing up the bridge—St. John was a port from which the war supplies from America to Great Britain could be shipped for use against the Germans.

But trust the people in a country town to catalogue a stranger. Horn went directly from the train about his errand; which was reckoning without the

Misses Hunter and the twelve-year-old Armstrong boy. They saw him toiling through the snow, marked the unusual weight of his suitcase from the way he carried it, saw him hide it in the woodpile by the siding—and then they talked. Soon Mr. Hunter hurried to the Immigration Station and told an inspector there about the suspicious stranger. The inspector hurried down the railroad track and met Horn returning from the international bridge that spans the St. Croix River a few hundred feet away. He asked where the stranger was going. Horn's reply was to ask the way to a hotel. When his name was next demanded he gave it as Olaf Hoorn, and said he was a Dane. The inspector then asked what he was in town for, and Horn said he was going to buy a farm. And, finally, the inspector asked him where he came from. When Horn explained in detail that he had come from New York via Boston the inspector, with a true legal mind, decided that he "had no jurisdiction," and let it go at that. His concern in life was with "immigrants" from Canada—and this man had proved that he had come from "an interior point." Hence he could do nothing officially, for the moment.

But the Misses Hunter's sharp eyes saw the stranger, after this interview, recover the suitcase from the woodpile before going on to Tague's Vanceboro Exchange Hotel for the night. The host at the hotel was not on duty when Horn registered, and never saw his baggage, but his mother, who happened to have occasion to enter Horn's room in his absence on the following Monday, noticed the suitcase, tried to lift it, and wondered how any one could carry it. Horn was a marked man from the moment he arrived in the town.

Evidently he sensed the suspicions he aroused, for he made no effort to proceed about his business that night, or the next. But shortly before eight o'clock on Monday night Horn gave up his room and said he was going to Boston on the eight o'clock train. He took his suitcase and disappeared. Instead of going to the station, he hid out in the woods until the last train for the night should go by. At eleven he was encountered in the railroad cut above the bridge by an employee of the Maine Central Railroad, who got such unsatisfactory answers to his questions that he talked the matter over with a fellow workman in the roundhouse, though without results. So Werner Horn marched out alone upon the bridge—alone except for his cigar and his suitcase, the spirit of the Fatherland upon him and the lying words of Von Papen in his ears.

He had need of the fire of patriotism to warm his blood and to steel his courageous spirit. It was a black winter night. The mercury was at thirty degrees below zero, the wind was blowing at eighty miles an hour, the ice was thick upon the cross-ties beneath his stumbling feet. The fine snow, like grains of flying sand, cut his skin in the gale.

But Werner Horn was a patriot and a brave man. Von Papen had told him that over these rails flowed a tide of death to Germans—not only guns and shells, but dum-dum bullets that added agony to death. He must do his bit to save his fellow soldiers; must help to stop the tide. Destroy this bridge, and for a time at least the cargoes would be kept from St. John and Halifax. It was a short bridge, but a strategic one, and the most accessible. So Horn stumbled on. He must get beyond the middle. Von Papen had not urged it, but Werner Horn had balked about this business from the first—not through lack of courage (he would go as a soldier upon the enemy's territory and there fire his single shot at any risk against their millions), but he would not commit a crime for anybody, not even for the Kaiser; nor would he trespass on the soil of hospitable America. Hence on each sleeve he wore the colours of his country: three bands, of red and white and black. Von Papen had beguiled him into thinking these transformed him from a civilian to a soldier. Twice as he struggled through the darkness he slipped and fell, barely saving himself from death on the ice below. Each time he clung doggedly to his suitcase full of dynamite.

Suddenly a whistle shrieked behind him, and in a moment the glaring eyes of an express train's locomotive shone upon him. Horn clutched with one hand at a steel rod of the bridge and swung out over black nothingness, holding the suitcase safe behind him with the other. The train thundered by, and left him painfully to recover his uncertain footing on the bridge. The second of Von Papen's lies had been disproven.

He had promised Horn that the last train for the night would have been gone at this hour, for Horn had said he would do nothing that would put human lives in peril. But Horn thought only that Von Papen had misunderstood the schedules.

A few moments after he had got this shock, another whistle screamed at him from the Canadian shore, and again he made his quick, precarious escape by hanging out above the river by one hand and one foot. He now decided that all schedules had been put awry, and that he must change his plans to be sure of not endangering human beings. To accomplish this, he cut off and threw away most of the fifty-minute fuse that he had brought along, and left only enough to burn three minutes. No train would come sooner than this, and then the explosion would warn everybody of the danger.

In doing this, Horn deliberately cut himself off from hope of escaping capture. He had planned such an escape—an ingenious plan, too, except that it was traced on a railroad time-table map of the Maine woods in winter by a strange German fresh from the tropics. He had meant to walk back one station westward, then cut across the open country to the end of a branch line railroad, and then ride back to Boston on another line than that on which he had come east to Vanceboro. It was a clever scheme, except that it missed all the essentials, such as the thirty miles of trackless woods, the snow feet-deep upon the level, the darkness of winter nights, and the deadly cold. Still, Horn childishly believed it feasible, and he did a brave and honourable thing to throw it overboard rather than to cause the death of innocent people.

He fixed the dynamite against a girder of the bridge above the Canadian bank of the river, adjusted the explosive cap, and touched his cigar to the end of the three-minute fuse. Then he stumbled back across the gale-swept, icy bridge, made no effort to escape, and walked back into the hotel in Vanceboro, with both hands frozen, as well as his ears, his feet, and his nose. A moment after he entered the hotel the dynamite exploded with a report that broke the windows in half the houses in the town and twisted rods and girders on the bridge sufficiently to make it unsafe but not enough to ruin it.

Everybody in Vanceboro was aroused. Host Tague, of the Exchange Hotel, leaped from his bed and looked out of the window. Seeing nothing, he struck a light and looked at his watch, which said 1:10, and then he hurried into the hall, headed for the cellar, to see if his boiler had exploded. In the hall he faced the bathroom. There stood Werner Horn, who mildly said "Good morning" to his astonished host. Tague returned the greeting and went back to get his clothes on. He had surmised the truth, and Horn's connection with it. When he came back out into the hall, Horn was still in the bathroom, and said: "I freeze my hands." Small wonder, after five hours in that bitter gale. Tague opened the bathroom window and gave him some snow to rub on his frozen fingers, and then hurried to the bridge to see the damage. He found enough to make him press on to the station on the Canadian side, and then come back to Vanceboro, so that trains would be held from attempting to cross it.

When he got back to his hotel, Horn asked to have again the room he had given up that evening. Tague had let it to another guest, but gave Horn a room on the third floor. There the German turned in and went to sleep.

Meanwhile, human nature as artless as Werner Horn's was at work in Vanceboro. The chief officer of law thereabouts was "John Doe," a deputy sheriff, chief fish and game warden, and licensed detective for the state of Maine. His later testimony doubtless would have had a sympathetic reader in the Man in Lower 3 (if only he had known): "I was asleep at my home, which is about three or four hundred feet from the bridge; heard a noise about 1:10 A. M., which I thought was an earthquake, a collision of engines, or a boiler explosion in the heating plant. The noise disturbed me so that I could not get to sleep. (And the Man in Lower 3 slept on!) I got up in the morning at about half-past five; met a man who said they had blown up the bridge."

But while Mr. Doe was about his disturbed slumbers, the superintendent of the Maine Central Railroad was making a Sheridan's Ride through the night by special train from Mattawamkeag, fifty miles away. He, at least, was on the job—he had brought along a claim agent of the road, to take care of damage suits. When they reached the Vanceboro station, they sent for Mr. Doe, and when he arrived at seven o'clock, Canada also was represented by two constables in uniform. This being a case for Law and not for Commerce, Mr. Doe took charge. He told the others that the first thing to do was to cover all the stations by telegraph and arrest all suspicious parties. Then he led his posse to the hotel.

There Mr. Tague told them about the German peacefully asleep upstairs. He led them to the upper floor and pointed out the room, but went no farther, as he thought there might be shooting. His sister, being of the same mind, sought the cellar. Doe knocked upon the door.

"What do you want?" called Werner Horn.

"Open the door," commanded Doe.

The door swung open, and the big German sat back on his bed. Then he saw the Canadian uniforms and jumped for his coat. Doe shoved him back, and one of the constables got the coat, and the revolver in it. When Doe told Horn he was an American officer, Horn stopped resisting and said:

"That's all right, then. I thought you were all Canadians. I wouldn't harm any one from here."

Doe handcuffed Horn to his own arm and took him to the Immigration Station to make an inquiry. Here Horn told a straightforward story, but with one embellishment that caused more excitement than all the rest, and that ultimately revealed his own character in its clearest light. This story was that he had not brought the dynamite in his suitcase, but that, by prearrangement, he had carried the empty suitcase to the bridge and there met an Irishman from Canada, to whom he gave the password "Tommy," and that this Irishman had given him the explosive and then disappeared.

"Tommy" immediately became a sensation who overshadowed Horn himself. Canadian officers scoured the Canadian shore for days, looking for this dangerous renegade, and Americans were as zealous on our side of the river.

But Horn himself was in a dangerous position. Lynching bees were discussed on both sides of the river, and probably only prompt action by the local authorities prevented one. Both to hold Horn for more serious prosecution and to get him out of peril, he was charged in the local police court with malicious mischief in breaking the window glass in one of the houses in Vanceboro; he pleaded guilty and was at once removed to Machias, the county seat, to serve thirty days in jail. Five days after the explosion, the Department of Justice had Horn's signed confession, taken in person by the Chief of the Bureau of Investigation.

It was in the giving of this confession that Werner Horn revealed himself most fully as a patriot and a gentleman, and, all unconsciously, revealed that the cynical Von Papen was a liar, a cold-blooded criminal, and, for the second time in the first months of the war, the secret hand behind the violations of American neutrality instigated through him and Bernstorff at the behest of the Imperial German Government.

When the government agent saw Horn in jail at Machias, and warned him that what he said would be used against him in proceedings for his extradition into Canada, or prosecution here, Horn told the same straightforward story, with the same embellishment about "Tommy." "I met a white man," so Horn said, "whom I had never seen before, but who was about 35 or 40 years of age clean shaven—'Tommy'—I was told to say 'Tommy' when I met him—I cannot say anything that would involve the consulate or the embassy—Germany is at war—I received, however, an order which was from one who had a right to give it, a verbal order only—received it two or three days before leaving New York for Vanceboro."

Later he said: "I cannot speak of the rank of the man who gave the orders—I cannot even say that he was an officer. No one was present when the orders were given me in New York City. I cannot tell more because it was a matter for the Fatherland. I would rather go to Canada [where he knew they wanted to lynch him] than to tell more about my orders—this would be impossible—at least until after the war is over."

Horn admitted he had met Von Papen several times at the German Club in New York City, but no art could compel him to admit that he had got his orders from him. But, as the agent noticed, his manner gave his words the lie; and whenever he tried to tell anything that was inaccurate he did so with great difficulty and embarrassment. But finding him determined, at whatever risk, to withhold this information, and determined, too, to stick to the absurd story about "Tommy," the agent wrote out by typewriter a statement of the facts as he had given them for Horn to sign.

Horn read the statement over and said that he would sign it. Then the agent took out his pen, added a few items of new information, and wrote these words:

"I certify on my honour as a German officer that the foregoing statements are true," and handed Horn the pen to sign it. Horn read the last sentence and seemed nonplussed. He turned back through the pages of the statement, blushed, scratched his head, and finally grinned up at the agent with the one word:

"Tommy."

The agent grinned in turn:

"You mean it's all right except for Tommy?"

"Yes."

Horn would not sign a lie and pledge his honour it was truth. A close scrutiny of the cut further on will show where the period after the word "true" has been erased, so that the sentence could go on to say, before he signed it, "except as to 'Tommy'—that I did not buy the nitro-glycerine but received it in New York and took it with me in the suitcase. I cannot say from whom I received it. Werner Horn."

Ex. 1-J. H. M. Feb-24,1915 EXHIBIT "A"

Machias, Maine.
Feb., 7, 1915.

I, Werner Horn, after having been advised that my extradition to Canada has been asked by the Government of Great Britain and that anything I may say will or may beused against me in an extradition proceeding by the United States or in a prosecution by the United States if it shall be found that I have violated any of the laws of that country and that I may decline to talk at all or to answer any particular questions do voluntarily, willing and without any promises other than that my case will be dealt with by the United States fairly, impartially and in accordance with the law, make this statement.

I am thirty-seven years of age, a citizen of Germany and at the outbreak of the war was the manager of a coffee plantation in Guatemala, that I am an Over-lieutenant in the German ~~reserve~~ army, in inactive service having had ten years active service in the German army, that two hours after receiving the call to return for army service I was on my way. I went from Guatemala to Galveston, Texas, in August, 1914, remained there fourteen days, proceeded to New York City, waited there four weeks trying to get a steamer to return to Germany, found that this was impossible, started to Mexico, remaining en route 15 days in San Antonio, Texas, that in MexicoCity I received a card from the coffeeplantation in Guatemala that another man had my position, that I secured a position on an American coffee plantation, that about four hours before going from ~~to~~ Frontera to Villa de Aguas Chiapas I received a card that all German officers should proceed to Germany, that I returned on the same launch on which I had intended to go from ~~to~~ Frontera, ~~saw the German consul in Vera Cruz~~, sailed on a Norwegian steamer from Vera Cruz to New Orleans, was on the sea on Christmas day, arrived in New Orleans December 26, 1914, proceeded at once to New York by train, reported to the German Consul there either Jan ~~Dec.~~ 1 or 2, asked Captain von Papen if it was possible to go to Germany, he said that it was impossible, that I stayed at the Arietta Hotel on Arietta Street, Staten Island, three or four weeks and then went to Vanceboro, Maine.

WERNER HORN'S CONFESSION (first page)

6

I have had the flags I wore for about two years I got them when in Guatemala I got the suit case in a store that sells men's clothes-on the first floor. I bought the suit I am wearing for the trip on Staten Island across from the hotel and I bought the cap at the same place I had the overcoat which I bought at Wanamakers the day I got to New York from New Orleans I paid about $12 for the suit

I certify on my honor as a German officer that the foregoing statements are true except as to "Tommy" that I did not buy the nitroglycerin but received it in New York and took it with me in the suit case. I cannot say from whom I received it

Werner Horn

Witnesses.

G. E. Woodman
A. Bruce Bielaski

(last page)

In which he unintentionally revealed the guilty purposes of Von Papen to violate American neutrality and commit a crime against human life, and which Horn refused to sign upon his "honour as a German officer" until it was altered to remove the fantastic tale about a confederate in Canada. By looking closely the erasure of the period after the word "true" can be seen, made to permit this correction to be added.

If Werner Horn had been less honest, less humane, the black wickedness of his Imperial masters would have been less clearly visible. He was the one who was punctilious to respect American neutrality—while they flouted it. He was the one who risked his own life rather than imperil others—while they sat snug in Washington devising means to place on the rudders of American ships the bombs that would add another horrid chapter to their crimes. A mere criminal at Vanceboro might have been accused of exceeding their criminal instructions—Werner Horn refused to carry out the instructions they had given.

One cannot forbear to publish here a humorous incident in this case, in no way related to its immediate currents, but so characteristic of the American attitude in general at that time. Here was a drama of international politics, fertilizing the germs of war—the seeds of our own entrance into the conflict, with its present expenditures of billions in treasure and its prospective expenditure of human blood and tears. Into this epic picture walks a Yankee trader with a bottle of liniment for frost bite in his hand, and asks for a "testimonial." It is significant, because it was a faithful miniature of America at large in February, 1915—asleep to the perils of its "isolation," but wide awake to the main chance in war-begotten trade. Well could Von Papen and Von Bernstorff, well could the Kaiser in Berlin, afford to smile a little longer, and marvel again at a people still "so stupid."

But the American Government was on still other German plotters' trails. They were not asleep, nor stupid. Even while they went through the long, legal processes in which German intrigue tried in vain to save Werner Horn from delivery to Canadian justice (and Horn was supplied with good counsel and every facility for making his defence), among the Yankee traders there was alert activity as well as dormant patriotism. The way in which the Department of Justice, through these merchants, lawyers, doctors, men of the "main chance," soon had a network of special agents in every city, town, and hamlet in the country, is one of the cleverest pieces of American Government detective work born of the war.

CHAPTER III
Robert Fay and the Ship Bombs

Robert Fay landed in New York on April 23, 1915. He landed in jail just six months and one day later—on October 24th. In those six months he slowly perfected one of the most infernal devices that ever emerged from the mind of man. He painfully had it manufactured piece by piece. With true German thoroughness he covered his trail at every point—excepting one. And five days after he had aroused suspicion at that point, he and his entire group of fellow conspirators were in jail. The agents of American justice who put him there had unravelled his whole ingenious scheme and had evidence enough to have sent him to the penitentiary for life if laws since passed had then been in effect.

Only the mind that conceived the sinking of the *Lusitania* could have improved upon the devilish device which Robert Fay invented and had ready for use when he was arrested. It was a box containing forty pounds of trinitrotoluol, to be fastened to the rudder post of a vessel, and so geared to the rudder itself that its oscillations would slowly release the catch of a spring, which would then drive home the firing pin and cause an explosion that would instantly tear off the whole stern of the ship, sinking it in mid-ocean in a few minutes. Experts in mechanics and experts in explosives and experts in shipbuilding all tested the machine, and all agreed that it was perfect for the work which Fay had planned that it should do.

Fay had three of these machines completed, he had others in course of construction, he had bought and tested the explosive to go into them, he had cruised New York harbour in a motor boat and proved by experience that he could attach them undetected where he wished, and he had the names and sailing dates of the vessels that he meant to sink without a trace. Only one little link that broke—and the quick and thorough work of American justice—robbed him of another Iron Cross besides the one he wore. That link—but that comes later in the story.

Fay and his device came straight from the heart of the German Army, with the approval and the money of his government behind him. He, like Werner Horn, came originally from Cologne; but they were very different men. Where Horn was almost childishly simple, Fay's mind was subtle and quick to an extraordinary degree. Where Horn had been humane to the point of risking his life to save others, Fay had spent months in a cold-blooded solution of a complex problem in destruction that he knew certainly involved a horrible death for dozens, and more likely hundreds, of helpless human beings. Horn refused to swear to a lie even where the lie was a matter of no great moment. Fay told at his trial a story so ingenious that it would have done credit to a novelist and would have been wholly convincing if other evidence had not disproved the substance of it. The truth of the case runs like this:

Fay was in Germany when the war broke out and was sent to the Vosges Mountains in the early days of the conflict. Soon men were needed in the Champagne sector, and Fay was transferred to that front. Here he saw some of the bitterest fighting of the war, and here he led a detachment of Germans in a surprise attack on a trench full of Frenchmen in superior force. His success in this dangerous business won him an Iron Cross of the second class. During these days the superiority of the Allied artillery over the German caused the Germans great distress, and they became very bitter when they realized, from a study of the shells that exploded around them, how much of this superiority was due to the material that came from the United States for use by the French and British guns. Fay's ingenious mind formed a scheme to stop this supply, and he put his plan before his superior officers. The result was that, in a few weeks, he left the army and left Germany, armed with passports and $3,500 in American money, bound for the United States on the steamer *Rotterdam*. He reached New York on April 23, 1915.

One of Fay's qualifications for the task he had set for himself was his familiarity with the English language and with the United States. He had come to America in 1902, spending a few months on a farm in Manitoba and then going on to Chicago, where he had worked for several years for the J. I. Case Machinery Company, makers of agricultural implements. During these years, Fay was taking an extended correspondence school course in electrical and steam engineering, so that altogether he had good technical background for the events of 1915. In 1906, he went back to Germany.

What he may have lacked in technical equipment, Fay made up by the first connection he made when he reached New York in 1915. The first man he looked up was Walter Scholz, his brother-in-law, who had been in this country for four years and who was a civil engineer who had worked here chiefly as a draftsman—part of the time for the Lackawanna Railroad—and who had studied mechanical engineering on the side. When Fay arrived, Scholz had been out of a job in his own profession and was working on a rich man's estate in Connecticut. Fay, armed with plenty of money and his big idea, got Scholz to go into the scheme with him, and the two were soon living together in a boarding house at 28 Fourth Street, Weehawken, across the river from uptown New York.

To conceal the true nature of their operations they hired a small building on Main Street and put a sign over the door announcing themselves in business as "The Riverside Garage." They added verisimilitude to this scheme by buying a second-hand car in bad condition and dismantling it, scattering the parts around the room so that it would look as if they were engaged in making repairs. Every once in a while they would shift these parts about so as to alter the appearance of the place. However, they did not accept any business—whenever a man took the sign at its face value and came in asking to have work done, Fay or Scholz would take him to a near-by saloon and buy him a few drinks and pass him along, referring him to some other garage.

The most of their time they spent about the real business in hand. They took care to have the windows of their room in the boarding house heavily curtained to keep out prying eyes, and here, under a student lamp, they spent hours over mechanical drawings which were afterward produced in evidence at the trial of their case. The mechanism that Fay had conceived was carefully perfected on paper, and then they confronted the task of getting the machinery assembled. Some of the parts were standard—that is, they could be bought at any big hardware store. Others, however, were peculiar to this device and had to be made to order from the drawings. They had the tanks made by a sheet-metal worker named Ignatz Schiering, at 344 West 42nd Street, New York. Scholz went to him with a drawing, telling him that it was for a gasolene tank for a motor boat. Scholz made several trips to the shop to supervise some of the details of the construction and once to order more tanks of a new size and shape.

At the same time Scholz went to Bernard McMillan, doing business under the name of McMillan & Werner, 81 Centre Street, New York, to have him make special kinds of wheels and gears for the internal mechanism of the bomb, from sketches which Scholz supplied. At odd times between June 10th and October 20th McMillan was working on these things and delivered the last of them to Scholz just a few days before he was arrested.

In the meanwhile, Fay was taking care of the other necessary elements of his scheme. Besides the mechanism of the bomb, he had to become familiar with the shipping in the port of New York, and he had to get the explosive with which to charge the bomb. For the former purpose he and Scholz bought a motor boat—a 28-footer—and in this they cruised about New York harbour at odd times, studying the docks at which ships were being loaded with supplies for the Allies and calculating the best means and time for placing the bombs on the rudder posts of these ships. Fay finally determined by experience that between two and three o'clock in the morning was the best time. The watchmen on board the ships were at that hour most likely to be asleep or the night dark enough so that he could work in safety. He made some actual experiments in fastening the empty tanks to the rudder posts, and found that it was perfectly easy to do so. His scheme was to fasten them just above the water line on a ship while it was light, so that when it was loaded they were submerged and all possibility of detection was removed.

The getting of explosives was, however, the most difficult part of Fay's undertaking. This was true not only because he was here most likely to arouse suspicion, but also because of his relative lack of knowledge of the thing he was dealing with. He did know enough, however, to begin his search for explosives in the least suspicious field, and it was only as he became ambitious to produce a more powerful effect that he came to grief.

The material he decided to use at first was chlorate of potash. This substance in itself is so harmless that it is an ingredient of tooth powders and is used commonly in other ways. When, however, it is mixed with any substance high in carbons, such as sugar, sulphur, charcoal, or kerosene, it becomes an explosive of considerable power. Fay set about to get some of the chlorate.

But it is now time to get acquainted with Fay's fellow conspirators, and to follow them through the drama of human relationships that led to Fay's undoing. All these men were Germans—some of them German-Americans—and each in his own way was doing the work of the Kaiser in this country. Herbert Kienzle was a dealer in clocks with a store on Park Place, in New York. He had learned the business in his father's clock factory deep in the Black Forest in Germany and had come to this country years ago to go into the same business, getting his start by acting as agent for his father's factory over here. After the war broke out he had become obsessed with the wild tales which German propaganda had spread in this country about dum-dum bullets being shipped back for use against the soldiers of the Fatherland. He had brooded on the subject, had written very feelingly about it to the folks at home, and had prepared for distribution in the United States a pamphlet denouncing this traffic. Fay had heard of Kienzle before leaving Germany, and soon after he reached New York he got in touch with him as a man with a fellow feeling for the kind of work he was undertaking to do.

One of the first things in Fay's carefully worked-out plan was to locate a place to which he could quietly retire when his work of destruction should be done—a place where he felt he could be safe from suspicion. After a talk with Kienzle he decided that Lush's Sanatorium, at Butler, N. J., would serve the purpose. This sanatorium was run by Germans and Kienzle was well known there. Acting on a prearranged plan with Kienzle, Fay went to Butler and was met at the station by a man named Bronkhorst, who was in charge of the grounds at the sanatorium. They identified each other by prearranged signals and Fay made various arrangements, some of which are of importance later in the story.

Another friend of Kienzle's was Max Brietung, a young German employed by his uncle, E. N. Brietung, who was in the shipping business in New York. Young Brietung was consequently in a position to know at first hand about the movements of ships out of New York harbour. Brietung supplied Fay with the information he needed regarding which ships Fay should elect to destroy. But first Brietung made himself useful in another way.

Fay asked Kienzle how he could get some chlorate of potash, and Kienzle asked his young friend Brietung if he could help him out. Brietung said he could, and went at once to another German who was operating in New York ostensibly as a broker in copper under the name of Carl L. Oppegaard.

It is just as well to get better acquainted with Oppegaard because he was a vital link in Fay's undoing. His real name was Paul Siebs and for the purpose of this story he might as well be known by that name. Siebs had also been in this country in earlier days and during his residence in Chicago, from 1910 to 1913, he had gotten acquainted with young Brietung. He, too, had gone back to Germany before the war, but soon after it began he had come back to the United States under his false name, ostensibly as an agent of an electrical concern in Gothenburg, Sweden, for the purpose of buying copper. He frankly admitted later that this copper was intended for re-export to Germany to be used in the manufacture of munitions of war. He did not have much success in his enterprise and he was finally forced to make a living from hand to mouth by small business transactions of almost any kind. He could not afford a separate office, so he rented desk room in the office of the Whitehall Trading Company, a small subsidiary of the Raymond-Hadley Corporation. His desk was in the same room with the manager of the company, Carl L. Wettig.

When Brietung asked Siebs to buy him some chlorate of potash Siebs was delighted at the opportunity to make some money and immediately undertook the commission. He had been instructed to get a small amount, perhaps 200 pounds. He needed money so badly, however, that he was very glad to find that the smallest kegs of the chlorate of potash were 112 pounds each, and he ordered three kegs. He paid for them with money supplied by Brietung and took a delivery slip. Ultimately this delivery slip was presented by Scholz who appeared one day with a truck and driver and took the chemical away.

Fay and Scholz made some experiments with the chlorate of potash and Fay decided it was not strong enough to serve his purpose. He then determined to try dynamite. Again he wished to avoid suspicion and this time, after consultation with Kienzle, he recalled Bronkhorst down at the Lush Sanatorium in New Jersey. Bronkhorst, in his work as superintendent of the grounds at the sanatorium, was occasionally engaged in laying water mains in the rocky soil there, and for this purpose kept dynamite on hand. Fay got a quantity of dynamite from him. Later, however, he decided that he wanted a still more powerful explosive.

Again he applied to Kienzle, and this time Kienzle got in touch with Siebs direct. By prearrangement, Kienzle and Siebs met Fay underneath the Manhattan end of the Brooklyn Bridge, and there Siebs was introduced to Fay. They walked around City Hall Park together discussing the subject; and Fay, not knowing the name of what he was after, tried to make Siebs understand what explosive he wanted by describing its properties. Siebs finally realized that what Fay had in mind was trinitrotoluol, one of the three highest explosives known. Siebs finally undertook to get some of it for him, but pointed out to him the obvious difficulties of buying it in as small quantities as he wanted. It was easy enough to buy chlorate of potash because that was in common commercial use for many purposes. It was also easy to buy dynamite because that also is used in all quantities and for many purposes. But trinitrotoluol is too powerful for any but military use, and it is consequently handled only in large lots and practically invariably is made to the order of some government. However, Siebs had an idea and proceeded to act on it.

He went back to the Whitehall Trading Company, where he had desk room, and saw his fellow occupant, Carl Wettig. Wettig had been engaged in a small way in a brokerage business in war supplies, and had even taken a few small turns in the handling of explosives. Siebs had overheard him discussing with a customer the market price of trinitrotoluol some weeks before, and on this account thought possibly Wettig might help him out. When he put the proposition up to Wettig the latter agreed to do what he could to fill the order.

In the meanwhile Fay had sent another friend of Brietung's to Bridgeport to see if he could get trinitrotoluol in that great city of munitions. There he called upon another German who was running an employment agency—finding jobs for Austro-Hungarians who were working in the munitions plants, so that he could take them out of the plants and divert their labour from the making of war supplies for use against the Teutons. The only result of this visit was that Brietung's friend brought back some loaded rifle cartridges which ultimately were used in the bombs as caps to fire the charge. But otherwise his trip was of no use to Fay.

Carl Wettig was the weak link in Fay's chain of fortune. He did indeed secure the high explosive that Fay wanted, and was in other ways obliging. But he got the explosive from a source that would have given Fay heart failure if he had known of it, and he was obliging for reasons that Fay lived to regret. Siebs made his inquiry of Wettig on the 19th of October. The small quantity of explosives that he asked for aroused Wettig's suspicions and as soon as he promised to get it he went to the French Chamber of Commerce, near by, told them what he suspected, and asked to be put in touch with responsible police authorities under whose direction he wished to act in supplying the trinitrotoluol.

From that moment Fay, Siebs, and Kienzle were "waked up in the morning and put to bed at night" by detectives from the police department of New York City and operatives of the Secret Service of the United States. By arrangement with them Wettig obtained a keg containing 25 pounds of trinitrotoluol, and in the absence of Fay and Scholz from their boarding house in Weehawken, he delivered it personally to their room and left it on their dresser. He told Siebs he had delivered it and Siebs promptly set about collecting his commission from Fay.

Siebs had some difficulty in doing this, because Fay and Scholz, being unfamiliar with the use of the explosive, were unable to explode a sample of it and decided that it was no good. They had come home in the evening and found the keg on their dresser and had opened it. Inside they found the explosive in the form of loose white flakes. To keep it more safely, they poured it out into several small cloth bags. They then took a sample of it and tried by every means they could think of to explode it. They even laid some of it on an anvil and broke two or three hammers pounding on it, but could get no result. They then told Siebs that the stuff he had delivered was useless. Wettig volunteered to show them how it should be handled. Accordingly, he joined them the following day at their room in Weehawken and went with them out into the woods behind Fort Lee, taking along a small sample of the powder in a paper bag. In the woods the men picked up the top of a small tin can, built a fire in the stump of a tree, and melted some of the flake "T. N. T." in it. Before it cooled, Wettig embedded in it a mercury cap. When cooled after being melted, T. N. T. forms a solid mass resembling resin in appearance, and is now more powerful because more compact.

However, before the experiment could be concluded, one of the swarm of detectives who had followed them into the woods stepped on a dry twig, and when the men started at its crackling, the detectives concluded they had better make their arrests before the men might get away; and so all were taken into custody. A quick search of their boarding house, the garage, a storage warehouse in which Fay had stored some trunks, and the boathouse where the motor boat was stored, resulted in rounding up the entire paraphernalia that had been used in working out the whole plot. All the people connected with every phase of it were soon arrested.

Out of the stories these men told upon examination emerged not only the hideous perfection of the bomb itself, but the direct hand that the German Government and its agents in this country had in the scheme of putting it to its fiendish purpose. First of all appeared Fay's admission that he had left

Germany with money and a passport supplied by a man in the German Secret Service. Later, on the witness stand, when Fay had had time enough carefully to think out the most plausible story, he attempted to get away from this admission by claiming to have deserted from the German Army. He said that he had been financed in his exit from the German Empire by a group of business men who had put up a lot of money to back an automobile invention of his, which he had worked on before the war began. These men, so he claimed, were afraid they would lose all their money if he should happen to be killed before the invention was perfected. This tale, ingenious though it was, was too fantastic to be swallowed when taken in connection with all the things found in Fay's possession when he was arrested. Beyond all doubt his scheme to destroy ships was studied and approved by his military superiors in Germany before he left, and that scheme alone was his errand to this country.

Far less ingenious but equally damning was his attempt to explain away his relations with Von Papen. The sinister figure of the military attaché of the German Embassy at Washington leers from the background of all the German plots; and this case was no exception. It was known that Fay had had dealings with Von Papen in New York, and on the witness stand he felt called upon to explain them in a way that would clear the diplomatic service of participation in his evil doings. He declared that he had taken his invention to Von Papen and that Von Papen had resolutely refused to have anything to do with it. This would have been well enough if Fay's explanation had stopped here.

But Fay's evil genius prompted him to make his explanation more convincing by an elaboration of the story, so he gave Von Papen's reasons for refusal. These were not at all that the device was calculated to do murder upon hundreds of helpless men, nor at all that to have any part in the business was to play the unneutral villain under the cloak of diplomatic privilege. Not at all. At the first interview, seeing only a rough sketch and hearing only Fay's description of preliminary experiments, Von Papen's sole objection was:

"Well, you might obtain an explosion once and the next ten apparatuses might fail."

To continue Fay's explanation:

"He casually asked me what the cost of it would be and I told him in my estimation the cost would not be more than $20 apiece. [$20 apiece for the destruction of thirty lives and a million-dollar ship and cargo!] As a matter of fact, in Germany I will be able to get these things made for half that price. 'If it is not more than that,' Von Papen said, 'you might go ahead, but I cannot promise you anything whatever.'"

Fay then went back to his experiments and when he felt that he had practically perfected his device he called upon Von Papen for the second time. This time Von Papen's reply was:

"Well, this thing has been placed before our experts and also we have gone into the political condition of the whole suggestion. Now in the first place our experts say this apparatus is not at all seaworthy; but as regards political conditions I am sorry to say we cannot consider it and, therefore, we cannot consider the whole situation."

In other words, with no thought of the moral turpitude of the scheme, with no thought of the abuse of diplomatic freedom, but only with thoughts of the practicability of this device and of the effect upon political conditions of its use, Von Papen had put the question before technical men and before Von Bernstorff, and their decision had been adverse solely on those considerations—first, that it would not work, and second, that it would arouse hostility in the United States. At no stage, according to Fay's best face upon the matter, was any thought given to its character as a hideous crime.

The device itself was studied independently by two sets of military experts of the United States Government with these results:

First, that it was mechanically perfect; second, that it was practical under the conditions of adjustment to a ship's rudder which Fay had devised; and third, that the charge of trinitrotoluol, for which the container was designed, was nearly half the quantity which is used on our own floating mines and which is calculated upon explosion twenty feet from a battleship to put it out of action, and upon explosion in direct contact, absolutely to destroy and sink the heaviest superdreadnaught. In other words, beyond all question the bomb would have shattered the entire stern of any ship to which it was attached, and would have caused it to sink in a few minutes.

A brief description of the contrivance reveals the mechanical ingenuity and practical efficiency of Fay's bomb. A rod attached to the rudder, at every swing the rudder gave, turned up, by one notch, the first of the bevelled wheels within the bomb. After a certain number of revolutions of that wheel, it in turn gave one revolution to the next; and so on through the series. The last wheel was connected with the threaded cap around the upper end of the square bolt, and made this cap slowly unscrew, until at length the bolt dropped clear of it and yielded to the waiting pressure of the strong steel spring above. This pressure drove it downward and brought the sharp points at its lower end down on the caps of the two rifle cartridges fixed below it—like the blow of a rifle's hammer. The detonation from the explosion of these cartridges would set off a small charge of impregnated chlorate of potash, which in turn would fire the small charge of the more sluggish but stronger dynamite, and that in turn would explode the still more sluggish but tremendously more powerful trinitrotoluol.

The whole operation, once the spring was free, would take place in a flash; and instantly its deadly work would be accomplished.

Picture the scene that Fay had in his mind as he toiled his six laborious months upon this dark invention. He saw himself, in imagination, fixing his infernal box upon the rudder post of a ship loading at a dock in New York harbour. As the cargo weighed the ship down, the box would disappear beneath the water. At length the ship starts on its voyage, and, as the rudder swings her into the stream, the first beat in the slow, sure knell of death for ship and crew is clicked out by its very turning. Out upon the sea the shift of wind and blow of wave require a constant correction with the rudder to hold the true course forward. At every swing the helmsman unconsciously taps out another of the lurking beats of death. Somewhere in mid-ocean, perhaps at black midnight, in a driving storm, the patient mechanism hid below has turned the last of its calculated revolutions. The neckpiece from the bolt slips loose, the spring drives downward, there is a flash, a deafening explosion, and five minutes later a few mangled bodies and a chaos of floating wreckage are all that is left above the water's surface.

This is the hideous dream Fay dreamed in the methodical 180 days of his planning and experimenting in New York. This is the dream to realize which he was able to enlist the coöperation of half a dozen other Germans. This is the dream his superiors in Germany viewed with favour, and financed. This is the dream the sinister Von Papen encouraged and which he finally dismissed only because he believed it too good to be true. This is the dream Fay himself on the witness stand said he had thought of as "a good joke on the British."

In this picture of infernal imaginings the true character of German plottings in this country stands revealed. Ingenuity of conception characterized them, method and patience and painstaking made them perfect. Flawless logic, flawless mechanism. But on the human side, only the blackest passions and an utter disregard of human life; no thought of honour, no trace of human pity. It happened in the case of Fay that the agent himself was ruthless and deserved far more than what the limit of existing law was able to give him when he was convicted of his crimes. But through all the plots Von Papen, Von Bernstorff, and the Imperial German Government in Berlin were consistent. Their hand was at the helm of all, and the same ruthless grasping after domination of the world at any price led to the same barbarous code of conduct in them all.

CHAPTER IV
The Inside Story of the Captain of the "Eitel Friedrich"

Out of the black picture of the German depravity in fighting this war have emerged four or five dramatic episodes that have stirred the imagination of the world and appealed to the romantic and chivalric instincts even of Germany's enemies. The cruise of the *Emden* will always remain one of the glorious traditions of the sea. The knightly spirit of those German aviators who flew low over the bier of their fallen foe of the French cavalry of the clouds, and strewed flowers upon it, was in the spirit of the best that war produces. America was the scene of two such episodes. The first unexpected appearance of the *U-53* upon our shores, rising unheralded from the unsuspected waters, thrilled the sporting instinct of our people. But perhaps the most dramatic incident was the arrival of the *Prinz Eitel Friedrich.*

During the night of March 9–10, 1915, this gallant cruiser of the Kaiserliche Marine, slipped into the harbour at Norfolk, having run the British blockade of cruisers outside the three-mile limit, ending a career of six months as a commerce raider, recalling the feats of the *Alabama* in the Civil War. The *Eitel Friedrich* was soon interned for the period of the war and her officers and crew put under formal arrest. Even the British, whose fleet had been outwitted, gave their tribute of praise to the men who had taken their fair chance and had got away. Captain Max Thierichens and his crew became objects of admiration to the world. They were showered with felicitations, most of all, as was natural enough, from Germans and German-Americans.

That is the bright side of the picture—and no one, even now, would care to dim its lustre.

But even at his best the German of the ruling class seems tainted with the ineradicable nature of the beast. The world has long accepted the Latin affinity of Mars and Venus—perhaps too complacently, though not without reason—so it would not have been surprised if the gallant Thierichens had not measured up to the standards of a Galahad. Nevertheless, it had a right to expect that he would not descend to the level of a Caliban; and Thierichens fell below even that low standard.

Among the great quantities of letters of congratulation which Captain Thierichens received were many from German-American women. They were stirred by the brilliancy of his exploit: it was a ray of light in the gloom that had fallen on the Teuton peoples after the Battle of the Marne, when the rosy vision of quick victory had turned to the gray fog of a long, defensive war. These letters breathed the passionate loyalty of the German spirit to the Fatherland. To these women, Thierichens was the embodiment of the martial spirit of their race—the spirit of the sons they saw themselves in imagination sending forth to war. Some phrases from their letters strike the key:

It is a pleasure for us to help our German brothers, but I also understand that you, my dear brother, are waiting to come out from your predicament. How grand it is that you are receiving letters from the Fatherland. We don't hear anything. Can't write anything, as the letters are not being delivered. So far good news. It is wonderful. My heart is jumping with joy. I look with confidence in the future. I have to please so many; have so many times to defend my Germany, but I have an unlimited confidence in God and in the truth.

Again: Hold your head high and do not forget: "starlight itself is in the night and God does not forsake his own."

Their attitude was one of high patriotism and maternal solicitude. They sent him books and delicacies, scraps of news from Germany, and in every way sought to comfort and inspirit their hero.

Thierichens was indifferent to the lofty purpose of these letters. His mind was depraved by the social custom of military Germany by which men of the officer class are in youth taught to consider themselves above the moral law. He was quite aware of the kinship of all emotions, and he promptly undertook to change the direction of these currents of passion into a channel more pleasing to his tastes. It was not long until he had narrowed his correspondence chiefly to three women and of these more particularly to two. Of these latter one was a German servant girl of rather better than average understanding, and the other a kindergarten teacher in the Middle West, one twenty-five and the other forty-five years of age. Their correspondence in both cases started on an exalted plane. It ended in depravity unprintable. Only a reading of the complete series of Thierichens's letters to these women could give a full understanding of the heartlessness, the baseness, and the ingenuity with which this man, always playing upon their patriotic fervour, transmuted their finer feelings into the most degrading travesty of romantic love. He and the kindergarten teacher never met. But by the time their correspondence came under Government censorship it had become a blend of exalted patriotism and of passion perverted to the obscenities pictured on the walls of ruined Pompeii.

Terrible as was the plight to which the teacher had descended, the case in which the German servant found herself was infinitely worse. Thierichens and she had met after their first interchange of letters and they had entered on a liaison of a character that became so base it cannot even be suggested.

All this while Thierichens was in correspondence with at least eight other misguided women. Fortunately for them the strong hand of the law intervened and Thierichens to-day is safely behind prison bars for his crimes. In the midst of this promiscuous correspondence he was receiving letters of affection and devotion from his wife and children, two of which may well be reproduced to make clearer the depth to which he fell. One is from his little daughter Christel, the other from his wife. They are as follows:

Kiel, November 26, 1916.

My Dear Father:

My darling, to-day the day of my 6th birthday, I will thank you all alone for the pretty things, lovely kisses for same. I hope my next birthday you will be with us again. I am praying every evening and morning to the dear

God that he will protect my dear father, and that the war will soon be ended, and you come again to the dear Fatherland.

Many hundred thousand kisses sent you,

Your thankful daughter,
CHRISTEL.

Kiel, Germany, 23rd March, 1917.

My Only Muckicken:

I want to chat with you again a little to-day; had very little time yesterday; did some shopping morning, and some stocking mending in the afternoon; some linen work in the evening; went early to bed; had love pains; had a little cold. This morning I went with Christel to Karestadt, bought some stockings, a school hat and gloves for her; also a leather hat for Elly; very neat. I am dressing Elly still like a child; she also is still wearing her hair down her back; she is any way a child yet. To-morrow I will get some bones from the war kitchen for Fritz, and then I shall ride together with the children to Aunt Niemann. To-day is a sunny day, but still a little cold. And now I shall answer No. 50. From Christmas Eve, 24–12–16. No, darling, we want to hope that we shall enjoy the 6th Christmas evening together; a description of our Christmas evening you probably received. You darling, you're writing so as if we were hungry, no, my darling, we have not had any hunger here in Germany yet. We are having our butter, eggs, meat, bread, and potatoes every day; only not so much of it as in times of peace. Well, of course, then everything was extravagantly used. So now everybody has to learn to be economical which is a good lesson for days to come, so please don't listen to the talk of our enemies,—we are all right; nobody will conquer us; God, the Lord, won't leave us alone,—we are all brave. What did Russia gain by the revolution? Something of that kind is impossible in Germany. The responsibility for same rests with England again. We shall wait to see how everything turns out. England will be punished surely. Now, my darling, enough for to-day.

Please remain healthy, and retain your humor. Be thankful and bravely greeted from your three sprouts and THIERE.

To make complete the picture of this hero of the Prussian officer class, it may be well to quote also the round robin of the crew of the *Prinz Eitel Friedrich*. To them even the air of an American internment camp was the breath of freedom compared to their service on a ship of his Imperial Majesty's Marine. Here is their opinion of life in it and of their gallant captain:

Fort Oglethorpe, Ga.,
July 8.

United States District Attorney,
PHILADELPHIA, PA.
Dear Sir:

We of the crew of the *Prince Eitel Friedrich*, beg to inform you about the conditions as there had been existing on board said vessel, and of the character of Captain Max Thierichens. He is one of the most cruel and dishonest men who ever had been in charge of a vessel. He is a disgrace to any military organization, and we feel ashamed that he brought disgrace to our vessel. He is one of the worst egoists in existence, without any feeling for his fellowmen. He is guilty of using the United States mails for fraudulent purposes, advertising in the papers that he would receive *liebesgaben* (love packages) for the soldiers in order to benefit himself, and later selling the same in the cantine after an inspection and rifling; he kept everything of value. He has received 1,000 of packages and money from very near every German society and countless private people, but his men never saw a penny of the same. The money he has spent for himself and some of his officers in his orgies.

As we had been out on the high seas, he only had an eye for his personal welfare. If we met a vessel, after stopping the same, the first thing he always did was to secure as much wine and other good things for himself, and officers, so that they always had plenty. He would not allow his sailors to bring enough potatoes and common food on board to satisfy their hunger. There had been cases where men had been severe punished just for taking a piece of meat from the table of one of the sunken vessels. The men did not even have drinking water but he and his officers used the same for bathing. He had been afraid that the U. S. Government would find out about his various misdeeds, so in order to make the Government think that he was all he should have represented he pulled off the biggest bluff ever thought of. He told ten men that they could run off, supplied the same with money, and after a few moments sent some other boys over the side to make as much noise as possible to call the attention of the guards. He had his men maltreated wherever there was a chance to do so. He even did this after we had been brought to Fort Oglethorpe. We have to thank the U. S. Officers for putting a stop to it. The captain had been mad that he lost the power over the men. He swore he would bring the men to a military prison for years to come, simply because they refused to be treated like dogs after being informed by the U. S. Officers that they don't have to stand for anything like that. If it was not for the iron discipline maintained by the Germans, there would have been a mutiny on board the ship. Even a common man hates to see good supplies going to waste just because the captain could not get quick enough to his wine, and the men feed on hardtack that was full of worms. Some of the men are willing to appear in court against the captain to bear out because they are not protected by the U. S. Government, and may have to face a court martial law if they are returned to Germany. We do hope that there will be an investigation of the evil doings of said Captain. If found guilty, we do hope that he may find out what it does mean to do wrong to his fellowmen.

CHAPTER V

James J. F. Archibald and His Pro-German Activities

The case of James J. F. Archibald, war correspondent, is another sample of the Germans' fatal gift for trusting a weak link in an otherwise ingenious and complete chain. Their "cleverness" was the cleverness of the cocky boy who thinks he can outwit any one. The sad ending of Archibald's career, the ignominious exposure of his character as a messenger for the Germans, was simplicity itself. And the revelations contained in the messages he carried were most discreditable to the honour and the wisdom of the plotters in the Teutonic embassies.

The story begins on July 29, 1914, six days after Austria's ultimatum to Serbia and three days before the formal historical date of the opening of the war. On that day an enterprising American newspaper syndicate telegraphed Mr. Archibald as follows:

Please telegraph us your terms for going to the European war, so that we can size up the syndicate field. As soon as received will try for quick action.

The Wheeler Syndicate, Inc.

Archibald soon had his arrangements made, though his employers were ignorant of the reason for the surprising ease with which he obtained the highest possible *entrée* to the best possible points of observation within the German lines. It should be said at once that their attitude was perfectly correct and that the moment they discovered the true nature of his errand they discharged him by cable, on October 27th. But that comes later in the story.

Archibald was a man of true grandiose German style. Writing to the syndicate on September 4th he said:

You should not confound my efforts with more than five hundred correspondents of every description who have attempted to get to the English, French, and Belgian fronts, none of them with any official recognition and most of them without even a passport. At the hysterical beginning of the war, correspondents are very much in the way but every cartoonist, humorist, and amateur millionaire who wanted a little private excitement rushed to the front and embarrassed the armies in their mobilization and naturally they were not gladly received. I have been working quietly, just as I did in the Russian War when I was the first, and only, foreign correspondent to be accepted after four months' waiting.

There is no necessity of coming into conflict with any censors if one knows military censorship as I do, for all they require is that you will not embarrass their present actual movements. There is not one single foreign correspondent with either the German or Austrian armies, and it will be a great achievement to get dispatches out from there and I am positive, with the papers that I now hold, that there will be no difficulty whatever. The difficulty is merely in establishing one's responsibility with these armies, and my residence in Washington for the last ten years has been for that purpose alone.

Archibald was soon in Germany and began sending back cable dispatches to a syndicate of papers, the principal ones of which were the New York *Times*, *Tribune*, and *World*. His dispatches, however, were so blatantly pro-German and had so much more propaganda than news in them that these papers quickly became dissatisfied. For example, the *Times* cut out of one of his dispatches a large section of fulsome eulogy of the German Government. Imagine their astonishment the next morning to receive a telephone call from Captain Boy-Ed, the Naval Attaché of the German Embassy with offices in New York. Captain Boy-Ed demanded the reason for the omission of these paragraphs. The *Times* naturally demanded Captain Boy-Ed's source of information that such paragraphs existed. It soon developed that Boy-Ed was receiving direct from Germany duplicates of all the material that Archibald was cabling for publication. As soon as the American newspapers understood this situation they declined to proceed further. In the same spirit and simultaneously the Wheeler Syndicate "fired" Mr. Archibald by cable and wrote him a stinging letter from which the following two paragraphs may be quoted:

Perhaps because of the nature of your stuff, at any rate, we have to face the veiled insinuation that you are in the pay of the German and Austrian Governments. In this connection, we have been told that the German and Austrian Ambassadors to this country have received in skeleton form the several wireless dispatches you sent to us addressed care the *Times*. We think you should know this, and also know that, with the nature of your dispatches such as they were, we dared not allow ourselves, by continuing the service, to be laid open to the charge that we were in the employ of the German and Austrian Governments. So we had to terminate the service.

We have instructed the *Times* not to accept any more wireless dispatches from you, and the wireless company has been notified that no dispatches will be accepted. We regret exceedingly the situation, but it is one that has arisen solely from the fact that you have sent over your personal pro-German opinions instead of the battlefront news you assured us that you would furnish us.

Nothing daunted by these rebuffs, Archibald continued his exploits as "war correspondent," interspersing his labours at the front with voyages back to the United States, ostensibly to deliver lectures. The true character of his movements stands revealed in a letter Archibald received from Bernstorff, the German Ambassador, a few days before he embarked on the voyage from New York which was to be his last. This letter was written from Bernstorff's summer home at Cedarhurst, Long Island, on the 19th of August, 1915, and reads as follows:

Dear Mr. Archibald:

I send you herewith the two letters of recommendation asked for and hope that they will be useful to you. I learn with pleasure that you wish once again to return to Germany and Austria *as you have interceded for our concerns here so courageously and successfully*.

With best compliments,

Yours very sincerely,
BERNSTORFF.

One of these letters was as follows:

The German Frontier Custom Authorities are requested to kindly give to the bearer of this letter, Mr James J. F. Archibald, from New York, who is going to Germany with photographic apparatus, etc., in order to collect material for lectures in the United States *in the interests of Germany*, all possible facilities compatible with regulations in the dispatching of his luggage.

Imperial Ambassador
BERNSTORFF.

The familiar story of what happened next is that Archibald carried some secret documents for Bernstorff and Dumba in a hollow cane. This could scarcely be, for the documents he carried were so numerous and some of them so bulky that the cane would need to have been a giant's walking stick. In any event, the documents themselves are of more interest than their vehicle. They were taken from Archibald by the British authorities at Falmouth. The series can be best introduced by a letter from Ambassador Dumba to his chief, Baron Burian, Minister for Foreign Affairs in Vienna, which reads:

My Lord:

Yesterday evening Consul General von Nuber received the inclosed *aide mémoire* from the chief editor of the locally known paper, *Szabodsog*, after a previous conference with him and in pursuance of his proposals to arrange for strikes in the Bethlehem Schwab steel and munitions war factory, and also in the Middle West.

Dr. Archibald, who is well known to your lordship, leaves to-day at 12 o'clock on board the *Rotterdam*, for Berlin and Vienna. I take this rare and safe opportunity to warmly recommend the proposal to your lordship's favourable consideration.

It is my impression that we can disorganize and hold up for months, if not entirely prevent, the manufacture of munitions in Bethlehem and the Middle West, which, in the opinion of the German military attaché, is of great importance and amply outweighs the expenditure of money involved.

But even if strikes do not come off, it is probable that we should extort, under the pressure of the crisis, more favourable conditions of labour for our poor, down-trodden fellow countrymen. In Bethlehem these white slaves are now working for twelve hours a day and seven days a week. All weak persons succumb and become consumptives.

So far as German workmen are found among the skilled hands, a means of leaving will be provided for them.

Besides this a private German registry office has been established, which provided employment for persons who have voluntarily given up their places, and is already working well. They will also join, and the widest support is assured me.

I beg your excellency to be so good as to inform me with reference to this letter by wireless telegraphy, replying whether you agree.

Dumba.

The consideration which "Doctor" Archibald received for his complacency in giving his friends Dumba and Bernstorff "this rare and safe opportunity" is indicated by his receipt of April 24, 1915, to the German Embassy in Washington for $5,000 for propaganda work.

Further light upon "the enclosed *aide mémoire* ... in pursuance of his proposals to arrange for strikes in the Bethlehem Schwab steel and munitions war factory," is gained by the following quotations from the enclosure mentioned by Dumba in his letter to Burian. The enclosure was an outline of a scheme for fomenting strikes, submitted to Dumba by William Warm, the Editor of *Szabodsog* [in English, *Freedom*.]

In my opinion we must start a very strong agitation on this question in the *Freedom* (*Szabodsog*) a leading organ, with respect to the Bethlehem works and the conditions there. This can be done in two ways, and both must be utilized. In the first place, a regular daily section must be devoted to the conditions obtaining there and a campaign must be regularly conducted against those indescribably degrading conditions. The *Freedom* has already done something similar in the recent past, when the strike movement began at Bridgeport. It must naturally take the form of strong, deliberate, decided, and courageous action. Secondly, the writer of these lines would begin a labour novel in that newspaper much on the lines of Upton Sinclair's celebrated story, and this might be published in other local Hungarian, Slovak, and German newspapers also. Here we arrive at the point that naturally we shall also require other newspapers. The American *Magyar Nepszava* (Word of the People) will undoubtedly be compelled willingly or unwillingly to follow the movement initiated by the *Freedom* (*Szabodsog*), for it will be pleasing to the entire Hungarian element in America, and an absolute patriotic act to which that open journal (the *Nepszava*) could not adopt a hostile attitude....

In the interest of successful action at Bethlehem and the Middle West, besides the *Szabodsog*, the *Nepszava*, the new daily paper of Pittsburg must be set in motion, and those of Bridgeport, Youngtown District, etc., also two Slovak papers. Under these circumstances, the first necessity is money. To Bethlehem must be sent as many reliable Hungarian and German workmen as I can lay my hands on who will join the factories and begin their work in secret among their fellow workmen. For this purpose, I have my men Turners in Steelwork. We must send an organizer, who in the interests of the Union will begin the business in his own way. We must also send so-called "soap-box" orators who will know, and so to start a useful agitation. We shall want money for popular meetings and possibly for organizing picnics. In general, the same applies to the Middle West. I am thinking of Pittsburg and Cleveland in the first instance, as to which I could give details only if I were to return and spend at least a few days there.

It is my opinion that for the special object of starting the Bethlehem business and for the Bethlehem and Western newspaper campaign, $15,000 to $20,000 must be able to be disposed of, but it is not possible to reckon how much will ultimately be required; when a beginning has been made it will be possible to see how things develop, and where and how much it is worth while to spend. The above-mentioned preliminary sum would suffice to partially satisfy the demands of the necessary newspapers and to a considerable extent those of the Bethlehem campaign.

These documents should be read in the light of their date, August 20, 1915, and of the fact that the United States was a neutral nation, still harbouring the representatives of the "friendly" German and Austro-Hungarian empires. They are conclusive enough, in themselves, of the pernicious activities of these Embassies, but they wall become doubly significant in a later article in this series when they are read in the light of the activities of "Labour's National Peace Council."

Another document which Dumba entrusted to Archibald was his report to Burian on the then recent publication in the New York *World* of the papers taken from a satchel left in an elevated train by Dr. Heinrich Albert, the financial adviser of the German Embassy in America and the paymaster for a great deal of its work in plots and propaganda. This dispatch of Dumba's is worthy of reproduction in full. It is:

A map and a number of documents—typed but unfinished copies or statements of petitioners—were stolen from the financial adviser of the German Embassy here, obviously by the English Secret Service. These documents are now published in the current issue of the *World*, which has gone over to the English "Yingolager" (Jingo camp) as a great sensation, with cheap advertisement. The paper makes the most violent accusations against the German Embassy, mainly against Count Von Bernstorff, Military Attaché Captain Von Papen, and Geheimrat Albert, who are said to have conspired secretly against the safety of the United States, in that they have bought arms and munition factories, have concluded bogus contracts for delivery with France and Russia, have purchased large quantities of explosive materials, have incited strikes in the munition factories, have sought to corrupt the press, and have spread far-reaching agitation for the effecting of an embargo in the different American circles. The other important New York papers second the *World*, although with less violence, for, in their leading articles, by misrepresentation of the facts, they accuse Germany of all possible and impossible machinations—for instance, they, like the *World*, bring forward the assertion that the German Government wished to stop the supply of ammunition to the Allies, while itself secretly sending quantities over.

Count Von Bernstorff took the view that these calumnies were beneath reply, and by a happy inspiration, refused any explanation. He is in no way compromised. On the contrary, it appears from the published correspondence of various press agents that he vetoed the purchase of a press agency.

On the other hand, Geheimrat Albert published in the newspapers a very cleverly worded explanation, the tenor of which I venture to submit to Your Excellency in an enclosure. It is especially to the credit of the German Embassy that on July 15th last it informed the State Department officially that it found itself compelled to buy as many materials of war in this country as it possibly could, and to control their production, with the intention of preventing their being supplied to the enemy. These materials, it stated, were at any time at the disposal of the American Government at favourable prices, either as a whole or in parts, and of course this could only further the readiness of the United States for taking the field in war.

Here the absurd accusations of the conspiracy collapse. Also, with regard to the accusations as to the incitement of strikes, there is no proof of the empty statements made. Nevertheless, everything German here is slandered and run down with emphasis and consistency. An impartial individual can hardly escape the feeling of appreciation with which the far-reaching activity of Geheimrat Albert must inspire him. But there are very few impartial persons in New York.

The torpedoing of the *Arabic*, in the event of its having been done without warning, or its having caused American passengers to lose their lives, will do more than any newspaper accusations to prejudice Germany in the public opinion of the United States.

The Imperial and Royal Ambassador,
(Signed) C. DUMBA.

Archibald carried numerous other papers—for the Germans as well as for the Austrians. The most interesting of these was a report from Franz von Papen, military attaché of the German Embassy upon the same *World* exposure. The following are extracts from this dispatch:

Military Report
The "Sensational Revelations" of the New York *World*

On July 31 important papers were abstracted from Herr Geheimrat Dr. Albert in the elevated railway, apparently by an individual in the employ of the English Secret Service. These papers were sold to the *World* and formed the basis of the revelations (Enclosure 1) which gave to the New York press, friendly to the Allies, a welcome opportunity to make a fresh outburst against the Imperial Government and the Imperial representatives in this country....

Apart from political results the consequences of the publications for us show themselves in connection with business.

Bridgeport Projectile Co.

The report of June 30 of the Treasurer of this Company which I forwarded to the Royal Ministry of War on July 13, J. No. 1888, was among the stolen papers.

The declaration, published in the papers, of the President of the Ætna Explosive Co. that he intended to throw up powder contracts with the Bridgeport Projectile Co. is of course only newspaper gossip and was already much weakened yesterday through a fresh explanation by the firm (Enclosure V).

In connection also with the delivery of presses, I do not believe that the manufacturers will place difficulties in our way because the careful drawing up of the contract excludes all attack on the Projectile Co. under the well-known Sherman Law, and the claim that the manufacturers had supposed the deliveries to be intended for the Allies—in other words, that the contracts had been obtained by us under false representations—offers a legal basis too weak to enable the persons who undertake delivery to risk the expense and results of a lawsuit.

The only actual damage consists in that the Russian and English committee have at once broken off their negotiations with the Bridgeport Projectile Co. and that thus our plans to cut off, by the acceptance and nondelivery of a shrapnel contract, other firms here from the possibility of beginning the furnishing of war material have come to nothing.

The purchase of phenol by Dr. Schweitzer of the Edison Co., which has at the same time been disclosed, is disposed of by the explanation published to the effect that this phenol is only to be worked up into medicine.

Most of all have our efforts for the purchase of liquid chlorine been interfered with, since the tying up through middlemen of the Castner Chemical Company, which is friendly to England, appears now to be out of the question.

I shall use the means placed at my disposal (information of Herr Grothen) for the purpose of arriving at an agreement with the Electro Bleaching

Company. The published negotiations for the acquisition of the Wright's patent is without importance, since on our behalf a judicial decision against the Curtiss Company so far as one can see, would not have been obtained.

Part of the significance of Von Papen's dispatch is his reference to the Bridgeport Projectile Company. Other documents in the possession of the United States Government demonstrate completely the ownership of this corporation by the Teutonic Allies. Hans Tauscher, the agent of Krupps and other German munition factories in this country, was in the habit of reporting direct to the War Ministry in Berlin as if he were its representative in this country—as indeed he was though not ostensibly so. Among other papers in the hands of the Government is a letter from the President of the Bridgeport Projectile Company, informing him that the company is being reorganized and that hereafter Mr. Tauscher will hold as trustee *only 60 per cent.* of the capital stock. Naturally Tauscher was not acting as trustee for anybody but his employers.

Another document, of little importance, is a letter Von Papen wrote to his wife and sent by Archibald. But two parts of it are interesting. After speaking again of the *World*, exposure he, says:

The answer of Albert I am sending you herewith so you can see how we defend ourselves. The document we drew up together yesterday.

But the bright spot for the Americans whose hospitality he was abusing lies in this:

How splendid in the East! I always say to these idiotic Yankees that they should shut their mouths and better still be full of admiration for all that heroism. My friends from the Army are in this respect quite different.

Papen's "friends from the Army" have, with a good many of "these idiotic Yankees," organized an army and are looking for Captain Franz again, this time over the top in France, with the determination to settle the question with his government on the battlefield.

CHAPTER VI
A Tale Told in Telegrams

One day in October, 1915, a good-looking young fellow wandered into the office of the United States Attorney at Detroit and inquired if the office was making any investigations into dynamite cases. His inquiry was odd enough of itself, but coupled with his personal appearance and his entirely unexpected arrival on the scene, it was doubly mysterious. Lewis J. Smith, as his name turned out to be, looked like a handsome, big, farmer's boy who had come to town and made a little money. He was well dressed in what he considered the style, and in conversation developed a winning smile and a very engaging and convincing personality. There was the fresh wholesomeness of country breeding about him that comported strangely with his guarded and mysterious talk of dynamite. The United States Attorney thought he must be a "little off," but referred him to the local agent of the Department of Justice.

To this agent Smith told at first an incoherent story. But the agent was tactful and sympathetic and by asking a question now and then and even more by refraining from asking questions at embarrassing moments, he drew out from Smith most of the details of one of the most dangerous German plots, incidentally exposing the organization of the German spy system west of the Mississippi River.

The story revealed by Smith and by the corroborative testimony in the subsequent investigation was this: Consul-General Bopp discovered that the California Powder Mills at Pinole, across the bay from San Francisco, was manufacturing powder for the use of the Russians on the Eastern Front in Europe, and that this powder was being shipped from Tacoma and Seattle to Vladivostok. One particularly large shipment was under way and he wanted to stop it. He employed C. C. Crowley, who had been for many years head detective for the Southern Pacific Railroad but lately discharged for grafting, to undertake this job along with several others. Crowley lived in the Hotel Gartland in San Francisco, and bought his cigars at a little German stand across the street. Through this German, who was also patronized by Smith, Crowley learned that Smith had been employed recently in the California Powder Mills but was out of a job. Crowley introduced himself to Smith and first gave him the task of going back to the mill and finding out exactly how the powder for Russia was being routed. He gave Smith several hundred dollars, and the next day Smith's former fellow employees were astonished to see him ride up to the works in an automobile, completely outfitted in new clothes and flourishing a roll of bills big enough to make them gasp. Smith soon found how the powder was packed and marked and also that it was being loaded on a big scow and would be towed by sea to Tacoma for loading there on ships for Vladivostok.

A few days later Crowley told Smith to go to Tacoma and register at the Donnelly Hotel, and that he would join him there, going by another train. There they would manufacture bombs of a type which Smith had devised, and Smith was to place these bombs on the ships that would carry the powder to Russia.

Smith took his wife to Tacoma. They registered at the Donnelly Hotel, but as they soon discovered they would have to spend some time in the city, they took an apartment. Smith and Crowley were constantly meeting and between them surveyed all the shipping in the harbour and found out when the boats would sail and what they were carrying. The barge load of powder from California was towed into the harbour while they were there, and anchored in midstream to await the lightering of its cargo to the trans-Pacific ships. These ships proved to be the *Kifuku Maru* and the *Shinsei Maru* (Japanese), the *Hazel Dollar*, an American boat flying the British flag, and the *Talthybius*, a British ship. Smith undertook to place bombs on all of them.

What Smith actually did was to visit small stores in Tacoma and near Seattle and buy regular commercial 40 per cent. dynamite in sticks, telling the storekeepers that he was clearing a farm and wanted the dynamite for use in blowing up stumps. He loaded a lot of it into an old suitcase and left Crowley one afternoon, telling him he was going to place this on one of the ships that night. Instead, he went out into the woods with it, cached it under a log, the position of which he fixed in memory by a big stump and a tree that had a big rock in its fork, then walked on down to the railroad track, carrying his suitcase, and later threw the suitcase away down an embankment. He reported to Crowley that he had not been able to get anything on the *Kifuku Maru*, which was the first to sail, but that he had "fixed" the *Hazel Dollar*, the *Shinsei Maru*, and the *Talthybius*.

"WHEN THE WATER GETS TO THE BOILERS"

The explosion of the boilers of one of the neutral merchant steamers sunk by the *Eitel Friedrich.*

Crowley, in the meantime, had been keeping in touch with the Germans in San Francisco. It had been arranged that all dealings with them were to be through Von Brincken. Crowley, on his part, kept in touch with his secretary, Mrs. Cornell, she communicating in person, or by telephone, with Von Brincken, and Von Brincken reporting to Bopp and getting further orders.

A great deal of the story from this point on is A Tale Told in Telegrams. The first of these telegrams, which figured in the subsequent trial, was dated Tacoma, May 13, 1915. It was addressed to Crowley who had not yet joined Smith. The message was:

Fine weather Kaifuku Box 244 five days.

S. Hotel Donnelly.

This message was, of course, from Smith and was in the crude code that had been agreed upon. "Fine weather" meant that everything was O. K. "Kaifuku" gave the name of the ship on which the powder would probably be carried. "Box 244" was the post-office address through which Smith could be reached, and "five days" was the probable sailing date of the *Kifuku.*

It so happened, however, that a few hours after Smith had sent this telegram Crowley arrived in Tacoma. Crowley was always full of fear that he would be detected, and he was afraid of the message that Smith had sent. He, therefore, immediately telegraphed to Mrs. Cornell to go to the Gartland Hotel in San Francisco and get this telegram, and telegraphed also to the hotel to give it to her when she called.

Between one and two o'clock in the morning of Sunday, May 30th (Decoration Day), everybody in Tacoma and Seattle was jarred from his slumbers by a terrific explosion in the harbour. The scow load of powder had disappeared in one grand flash, crash, and cloud of smoke, carrying with it the night watchman who had been living on it. One hundred thousand dollars' worth of plate glass in Tacoma and Seattle was destroyed and news of the explosion was telegraphed to the papers all over the country. Crowley had got the main part of his job done in one quick stroke.

Here was good news for the Germans. Crowley could not wait for the mails to carry it, so the next day he sent the following telegram to Mrs. Cornell:

Work has been good. And all fixed. No connection with the big Circus it was an accident to the Elephant.

C.

This cryptic message meant:

"Work has been good and all fixed," that he and Smith had had good luck in their plots against the ships and that bombs had been placed on all of them. "No connection with the big Circus it was an accident to the Elephant," the "big Circus" was the four ships for Vladivostok and the "Elephant" was the scow—in other words, the explosion had not interfered with their work against the ships.

Before Crowley got his message off, however, Mrs. Crowley had sent one to him. The Germans were in a panic. Von Brincken had telephoned her that Bopp had word that Smith had been arrested and had given the game away, so she telegraphed:

Von learned your friend told all before leaving. Anxious. Answer.

M. W. C.

To this Crowley replied:

Show that telegram to him also say I do not credit report on S. he made good.

C.

"That telegram" meant his message about the circus. To this Mrs. Cornell replied:

Don't understand your message. Get letter Portland Post-office on arrival.

M. W. C.

Crowley, she knew, was leaving immediately for San Francisco.

There were some grounds for the Germans apprehension. Smith was arrested and charged with having caused the explosion on the scow. But after a little manœuvring he managed to get free of the charge and, with money wired to him at Tacoma by Crowley, went back to San Francisco where Crowley paid him first $300 and then $600 in currency.

The Germans, however, had been pretty well frightened and they thought it was about time to get both Smith and Crowley away. Smith and his wife were hustled off to Sacramento where they lived at a hotel for a little while and then Mrs. Smith was sent on ahead to New York, while Crowley and Smith arranged to meet in Chicago to carry out a new plan that the Germans had devised.

This plot was to use Detroit as headquarters for operations in Canada and there to blow up the stockyards at St. Thomas, Ontario, and trains carrying horses for shipment to Europe. Crowley and Smith got together in Chicago and visited the stockyards to spot the shipments of horses toward the Atlantic seaboard. They learned that a good many of these shipments were being routed through Canada by way of Detroit. In the meantime, however, the Germans in San Francisco were getting restless. They had expected almost every day that the ships for Vladivostok would be reported blown up or missing. They had heard neither, and they were beginning to suspect that they had been deceived. They had been deceived, but so had Crowley—and this explains the tenor of his replies in the Second Tale Told in Telegrams. The first intimation of trouble he received was a telegram from Mrs. Cornell on June 21st, to which she signed her middle initial:

Saw him noon gave message. He was astonished. Said we'll suspend judgment for a few days. Queer news this morning. He suspects you were interested in the failure.

W.

Meantime, Crowley had gone on to Detroit and this message was wired to him at the Hotel Statler there. His reply is missing, but he evidently expressed astonishment at the message, giving some instructions for his office and asking for more particulars. To this message Mrs. Cornell replied:

Your instructions will be acted upon. Wired you first arrived.

W.

The second sentence of the message meant that the first boat, the *Shinsei Maru*, had arrived safely at Vladivostok, despite Crowley's previous assurances that it had been "fixed." This was what the Germans could not understand, and what had aroused their suspicions that Crowley had been deceiving them, and that he had possibly even been in somebody else's pay to "double cross" them. Their suspicions were redoubled, as seems natural enough in the light of Mrs. Cornell's message of June 29th to Crowley:

All three arrived. I am waiting your advice. Something queer.

In other words, the other two boats, the *Hazel Dollar* and the *Talthybius*, had safely made Vladivostok.

Meanwhile, Crowley had been having other troubles with Smith. One day he called for him at the Briggs Hotel in Chicago and found that he had disappeared. He learned that he had gone on to New York, leaving as his forwarding address simply "Station L, General Delivery, New York." Smith had two causes for anxiety. In the first place, he had not heard from his wife and did not know whether she had arrived safely. Consequently, on June 18th he had telegraphed to a friend in New York:

Can you give my wife's address. Important. Answer paid,

and received a reply the same day giving the address. He left Chicago at once and telegraphed her from Buffalo the following evening:

On train 36 Grand Central Depot 703 Sunday morning.

Lewis.

On Sunday afternoon Crowley telegraphed him from Chicago:

What is the matter? Was surprised when found you had gone. Send me some word to Stratford Hotel.

C. C. C.

Smith did not reply until four days later, after he had learned that Crowley had gone on from Chicago to Detroit. He then telegraphed him:

From Tacoma at Chicago. Address 308 East Fiftieth St., New York City.

S.

To Crowley the second sentence was plain enough, but the first one was unintelligible, so he wired Smith:

Do not understand message. Let me know if you are coming here. Important.

C.

Smith did not dare to explain by telegraph what the matter was, but he had become convinced that detectives were on his trail and that he had been followed all the way from Tacoma to Chicago. He had suddenly decided to give them the slip and temporarily to break his connection with Crowley until Crowley should be at a safer place for him to get in touch with him again. Also he wanted to "work" Crowley for some more money, consequently his reply on June 25th was:

Cannot explain by wire. Would come but finances don't permit. Can't find wife. Answer.

S.

The latter part of this message was another lie because he was with his wife at the time, but it served to excuse his absence and baited the hook for more money. Crowley promptly bit and replied:

I wired you fifty dollars. Come W. U.

C.

Corroborating this message was a service message of the Western Union operator to their New York Office at 24 Walker Street:

Send notice to L. J. Smith, 308 East 50 St. Report delay of transfer payable at Grand Central Terminal.

M. T. A.

This telegram authorized the payment of $50.

At the same time Crowley undertook to satisfy his German employers and to divert their minds from their previous disappointment by promising them some results on the new venture. He telegraphed Mrs. Cornell on June 25th:

Tell him I expect S. by Sunday then action.

C.

The "him" was Von Brincken and the "S" was, of course, Smith. The promised "action" was action in the plot to dynamite the cattle trains at St. Thomas, Ontario. The next day Smith was on his way to Detroit, sending a message on the train to his wife to let her know he was all right:

Arrived at Toledo O. K.

L.

Smith met Crowley in Detroit the following day and Crowley immediately telegraphed Mrs. Cornell further reassuring news for his German friends:

He arrived and will be in action in day or two. Weather cool. All O. K. Give all clippings to him let me know if any word from Hazel and friend. Let him know of S.

C.

This message meant that Smith had arrived and would dynamite the stockyards in a day or two, that there was nothing exciting to report, and everything was going well. The "action" referred to was the blowing up of the cattle trains and the St. Clair Tunnel at Port Huron. The "clippings" were newspaper reports of the explosion on the scow at Tacoma which he wanted Mrs. Cornell to give to "him" that is to Von Brincken. "Let him know of S" meant: "Tell Von Brincken that Smith is here." "Let me know if any word from Hazel and friend," meant that Crowley had not given up hope that there was a mistake about the ships having made Vladivostok in safety and that he expected still to hear that Hazel (that is the *Hazel Dollar*) and "friend" (*Talthybius*) had been destroyed.

The promised "action" was now, so Crowley thought, about to be produced. He was going to take Smith into Canada and cause some explosions. Consequently he telegraphed Mrs. Cornell on June 29th:

Night letter follows. Go to Toronto few days. Don't wire until Friday.

C.

This announced the approaching trip for action.

Crowley's scheme for "action" was this: Smith was to carry a suitcase full of dynamite and buy a ticket to St. Thomas, Ontario. Crowley was to carry a suitcase very similar in appearance, containing his travelling things, and was to buy a through ticket to Buffalo which would take him over the same route through Canada that Smith was to travel. This plan was actually worked out with one exception. Smith had a perfectly good imagination and a perfectly developed yellow streak in his courage. He still wanted the $300 monthly he was making and was determined to continue getting it, but he had no relish at all for the pictures conjured in his mind of what would happen to him if he were discovered in Canada with a suitcase full of dynamite. He showed the dynamite packed in the case to Crowley. Then he went out into the suburbs of Detroit, got rid of the dynamite and, from a night watchman on a brick building in course of construction, bought a half-dozen bricks with which he filled the suitcase. This Irishman was afterward discovered and readily recalled both Smith and the circumstances, as he had been both puzzled and amused at the idea of anybody buying bricks when he could easily have stolen them.

As they had arranged, Smith boarded the Michigan Central train at Detroit late Sunday afternoon on July the 4th, and took a seat in the day coach. Crowley, who did not walk with him but followed close behind, took the seat behind Smith. Each, of course, stowed his suitcase at his feet. In a few minutes Smith walked to the front end of the car for a drink of water, whereupon Crowley stepped out on the platform at the rear. Smith came back and took Crowley's seat. Crowley returned and took Smith's seat. Shortly after, the customs inspector came through the train with the conductor. His presence was the reason for this exchange of seats. As Crowley had a through ticket to Buffalo and would not leave the train, the customs inspector did not open his suitcase but simply pasted on it the through ticket label by which it would be identified by the other customs inspector who would board the train at Niagara Falls, when the train was about to reënter the United States at Buffalo. Hence the suitcase containing the supposed dynamite was not opened, and this was Crowley's plan. Crowley's own suitcase, now in the seat with Smith, was, of course, opened and examined. But it contained nothing but Crowley's personal belongings. An hour or so later the stratagem was repeated and Smith and Crowley resumed their original seats and got possession of their original baggage. Smith dropped off the train at St. Thomas at about eleven o'clock that night and Crowley went on through to Buffalo.

Smith's nerve was no better this time than it had been before. In St. Thomas he emptied the bricks out of his suitcase, bought some travelling things to replace them, and took the train on to New York. In the meantime, Crowley had been having his troubles with the anxious and irritated Germans in San Francisco. There was an interchange of messages based on his need for money and on a break in the chain of communication between him and Bopp. Von Brincken had been made very unhappy by Bopp, as the latter was in a furious rage over the failure of the earlier plot at Tacoma, and had accused Von Brincken of everything from embezzlement to treachery and had made his life so miserable that he was glad of an excuse to get out of San Francisco. The immediate occasion he made for his leaving was an opportunity he had to go to Tia Juana, Mexico, just across the border from California. As both Crowley and his representative Mrs. Cornell had been positively forbidden to communicate with Bopp, Crowley was at the moment considerably embarrassed by his inability to get in touch with headquarters. This explains the meaning of Mrs. Cornell's message of July 2d, addressed to Crowley at Detroit:

Am trying to find him. Waited to hear from you.

W.

She did manage to reach Von Brincken just before he left for Mexico late the same day, again telegraphing Crowley:

He said: If you have plans go ahead with them. State amount required. Have been looking for results.

W.

Crowley replied the next morning:

Tell him have planned action for within a week. No doubt able to make showing. Ans.

C.

His reply, however, was too late. Von Brincken had gone to Mexico, hence Mrs. Cornell telegraphed:

Cannot get in touch with him. Have tried everything. Wired you last night state amount required. Advise me.

W.

To this message Crowley replied:

Don't worry. Did he get night letter thirtyth? Go to Buffalo to-morrow night. Statler. If you find him wire me. Don't send money until decided.

C.

The following day was the Sunday on which Crowley and Smith left Detroit together. Smith dropped off at St. Thomas and Crowley proceeded to Buffalo. The following evening Crowley again telegraphed Mrs. Cornell from Buffalo:

Nothing from you. Send me long letter to-night.

C.

Her reply was:

Nothing from him since last Wednesday except one phone telling you state amount. Believe he is fighting for time. Don't commit yourself he has no authority. Told me he expected to take another position in a month as the atmosphere was intolerable. I gave up apartment Saturday morning. Will wire.

W.

Mrs. Cornell had been unable to reach Von Brincken for the very good reason that he was out of town. Her quotation of his remark that he "expected to take another position within a month" referred to Von Brincken's untenable position in the Consulate in San Francisco, and to his manœuvres to get himself transferred to the New York end of the German spy system with his friend Von Papen, with whom he had become quite chummy on a recent visit of Von Papen's to the Pacific Coast.

Two days later, however, Von Brincken had come back to San Francisco and Mrs. Cornell had a talk with him. Following this talk she telegraphed to Crowley, who was now in New York, stopping at the Wallick Hotel:

Manager informed Bradford that experiences made were discouraging that outlook of lawsuit was too poor to justify advances for appeal. He is willing to offer lawyer contingent fee depending upon success only. Bradford privately advises see his friend in New York at once. Will send night letter.

W.

In this message Mrs. Cornell dropped into the code they had agreed to use before Crowley left San Francisco. "Manager" was Bopp, the head German in San Francisco. "Bradford" was Von Brincken. The "lawsuit" was the plot. The "lawyer" was Smith. "Bradford's friend in New York" was Von Papen.

In her promised night letter Mrs. Cornell said:

I asked for a hundred. They refused let him have it. He was indignant at refusal but decided it would be best in the end as it would justify your seeing other party who had plenty. He hopes to work with you soon. Don't forget to boost him. He looks to you for help. I have not selected a home yet.

W.

The latter part of this message urges Crowley to recommend Von Brincken very strongly to Von Papen when he sees him in New York so that Von Papen will be sure to transfer Von Brincken to the eastern territory so he can get away from Bopp. The next day Crowley telegraphed Mrs. Cornell from New York:

Appointment for to-morrow. Outlook not good. Will wire. Tell him I expect them to settle for all up to time of return or commencement here.

C.

The appointment, of course, was with Von Papen, but Crowley was not very happy about it as he seemed to have been failing right along to get anywhere, and he had now been so much criticized from San Francisco that he became fearful that Bopp would shut down on his money. Mrs. Cornell now gave up hope of getting action. On July 10th she telegraphed him:

Wasting time trying get them through me. Communicate direct. He knows I want him but won't see me. Moved 305 A Steiner with Alice few days.

M. W. C.

Crowley in desperation telegraphed for money from his personal bank account and got back a telegraphic order from Mrs. Cornell for $125. He divided with Smith and then bought a ticket for San Francisco so that he could deal direct with Bopp. Following Von Brincken's suggestion he told Smith when he left to go and see Von Papen, and get the rest of his money from him. Smith went to the German Club, on Central Park South, and sent up a message to Von Papen to which he got the curt reply that Von Papen did not want to see anybody from San Francisco. He had not yet been informed by Von Brincken that Smith was a man he could use.

Smith was now very angry, and casting all discretion to the winds, telegraphed openly and directly to the German Consulate in San Francisco, addressing the message to Von Shack on the theory that having exhausted all approaches to Bopp and Von Brincken he would go after the one man who still might be reached:

Why dont you answer?

Smith.

Three days later Smith telegraphed to Crowley who, he knew, would now be in San Francisco:

Please advise office that I request immediate reply also transportation back to Frisco. I resist (resent) the treatment I have lately received for my faithful service. Answer.

L. J. Smith.

A few days later, telegraphing from an office on the Exposition Grounds, in San Francisco, Crowley sent a message to Smith in New York:

Two hundred to-morrow one hundred Tuesday both Postal. Come.

C.

Crowley had now managed to restore some degree of confidence in his work and Smith's, and had adopted his favourite method of diverting attention from past failures by setting forth a glowing prospectus of a new scheme. For a third time the Germans "bit." In his eagerness Crowley thereupon sent a rush message to Smith:

Come to San Francisco at once.

C.

Smith promptly replied:

Enroute to-night.

S.

He arrived in San Francisco six days later, telephoned to Crowley at the Gartland Hotel, and Crowley in turn telephoned to Bopp that Smith was on hand. That evening Crowley and Smith got together in Crowley's room and made out a statement of Smith's expenses. This statement was a work of art. At Crowley's suggestion Smith carefully "padded" the account so that they both made a handsome profit on that besides their salaries. They met Bopp in the Palace Hotel the following morning and he there paid the amount of the expense account, $845, in bills.

Bopp and Crowley told Smith that they would probably have more work for him to do and for him to go back East. He left San Francisco on July 28th, telegraphing when he started to his wife at Cedarhurst, L. I.:

Remain one more week then meet me at Detroit. Answer at once.

L. Occidental Hotel.

She replied that she would meet him as directed. Smith went on to Detroit and stopped first at the Normandie Hotel and then moved out to a boarding house.

In a couple of weeks Crowley had got further orders from Bopp and wrote a letter to Smith in Detroit, saying that Bopp would give $500 apiece for blowing up the powder works outside Gary, Ind., and Ishpeming, Mich., besides paying his salary of $300 a month and expenses. Before Smith had time to get the letter he got another telegram from Crowley:

The matter in my letter is off. Write me letter

C.

What had happened was: Bopp had decided that Smith could get better results by working in California where he was more familiar with the powder plants and where he would be more closely under his direction and not under Von Papen's direction. After a discussion with Crowley, Bopp had agreed to a plan to have Smith return to California and get a job again in the California Powder Mills at Pinole, now owned by the Hercules Powder Company, and cause an explosion there. Following this agreement Crowley telegraphed Smith on August 30th:

Delay in information you want also in getting Consent on other matter will know in few days and will advise you. Will recommend if you can get good title to place here and the one north you be given an amount. Round trip transportation be furnished no other expense allowed.

Garrett.

Crowley had used the name of Garrett several times and often received mail under this name at his hotel in San Francisco. The meat of this message was: "if you can, get good title to the one here" and "the one north." The "place here" was the California Powder Mills, and "the one north" was a powder mill of the Ætna Explosive Company outside Tacoma with which Smith was familiar as a result of his trip there at the time of the explosion on the scow.

On September 7th Crowley telegraphed Smith:

They cannot decide on matter.

C.

Smith waited a week for a decision and then wired Von Shack again:

I expect immediate and satisfactory answer from you. Crowley has my letter.

L. J. Smith.

The satisfactory answer did not come. The Germans in San Francisco had spent all they were willing to spend without getting any result. Smith got a job in an automobile factory in Detroit, and his wife returned to her vocation as a *masseuse* in a Turkish bath. Pretty soon they both began to "see things"—Mrs. Smith in particular. First she thought she saw Crowley following her in disguise on the street one night. Smith began to suspect also that they were being trailed by detectives in the employ of the Germans, and finally he feared both bodily harm and violence, and the possibility of the American Government having gotten wind of some of his activities and dogging his steps to arrest him. He finally decided that the safe thing to do was to turn State's evidence, and hence he wandered into the office of the United States Attorney and started various trains of investigation that ultimately sent Bopp, Crowley, Von Brincken, and Von Shack to two years in prison, and Mrs. Cornell to one year. Smith and his wife were given immunity for turning State's evidence.

CHAPTER VII
German Codes and Ciphers

Secrecy is, of course, the most important consideration in the German plots in this country. When Bernstorff wished to arrange with Berlin to give Bolo Pasha ten million francs to betray his country, he naturally did not write out his messages in plain English for every wireless station on both sides of the Atlantic to read them as they went through the air. He did, to be sure, write the messages in English, and they looked plain enough—and innocent enough—but they meant something very different from what they seemed to mean. And when it got down to the actual transfer of the money, another German agent in New York signed the messages, which likewise were not what they seemed.

Those messages were in *code*. (They are reproduced and explained in this chapter.)

Now *code* should not be confused with *cipher*. When some Hindus in New York, subsidized by Berlin, wished to write their plans to some other Hindus in San Francisco, concerning their common purpose of fomenting revolution against British rule in India, they wrote out messages that consisted entirely of groups of Arabic numerals.

Those messages were in *cipher*.

To any one but an expert, many code messages look simple and harmless, and cipher messages usually look unintelligible and suspicious. Yet, oddly enough, the cipher messages are by far the easier to make out. Indeed, unless you have a copy of the code, code messages can almost never be translated, whereas a straight cipher message can almost invariably be unraveled by an expert, if you give him enough time and material. Hence, by people who know the subject (and nobody had mastered it so thoroughly as the Germans), codes are used for secrecy, and ciphers are used simply as an added precaution and to *delay* the unraveling of a message if, by any chance, the enemy has gotten possession of a copy of the code.

German plot messages, therefore, are usually written out first in plain German, then coded, and the code then put into cipher. Such messages are called *enciphered code*.

For an enemy to get them to make sense, he has first to decipher them, and then decode them. Any expert can decipher them—in time. Decoding them is a very different matter.

Before taking up some of the German code and cipher messages that have been translated, with dramatic results, it will be well to discuss codes and ciphers in general.

A *code* is an arrangement by which two people agree, when exchanging messages, always to substitute certain words or symbols for the real words of the message. Thus, they might agree on these substitutions:

a	=	the
French ship	=	market
sailed from New York	=	price
sailed from Boston	=	quotation
to-day	=	Is
for Marseilles	=	any even number

for Bordeaux =

any number with a fraction

With such a code, a German spy in New York could cable a seemingly harmless message to a friend in Holland, such as:

"The market price is 110."

That would mean, of course:

"A French ship sailed from New York to-day for Marseilles."

Whereas a very slight change in wording:

"The market quotation is 110¾."

would mean:

"A French ship sailed from Boston to-day for Bordeaux."

Messages of that sort could be exchanged daily between a broker in Wall Street and a broker in Amsterdam, and, by the addition of a few more words, could be infinitely varied and would look like perfectly legitimate commercial correspondence. In fact, most international business before the war (the Government now requires that all messages appear in plain English) was carried on by coded cables which turned long messages into short groups of words that of themselves made gibberish. Several code books for business use were on the market, containing hundreds of pages of these arbitrary substitutions, which were useful, not for secrecy but for economy. A dozen words could be made to say what normally would require five hundred words.

Ciphers, however, have almost always been resorted to when secrecy was desired. This sounds like a contradiction. But people who are not experts use them because they think they are more secret, since they look so. And experts use them when they are concerned only with *temporary* secrecy. They use them, then, because cipher messages can be written and translated (by one's correspondent) without any equipment, like a code book, and much more rapidly than code. Thus, if a general in the field wishes to send a message ordering a colonel to advance in two hours, he sends it in cipher, because it would take the enemy more than two hours to decipher the message even if he intercepted it immediately, and because after the two hours have elapsed the information in the message would be of no value to him.

A *cipher* is the substitution of some symbol for a letter of the alphabet. The substituted symbol may be another letter—as writing *e* when you mean *a*. Or it may be a figure—as using 42 when you mean *m*. Or it may be an arbitrary sign—as * to mean *c*. In cipher, then, every word is spelled out, but the word *Washington* might be spelled x=‖½?!^:°B if you had agreed that

w = x   n = !

a = =   g = ^

s = || t = :

h = ½   o = °

i = ?   n = B

That is called a *substitution* cipher, because some other letter or symbol is arbitrarily substituted for every letter.

But another kind is called a *transposition* cipher, because in this the letters of the alphabet are simply transposed by agreement—the simplest and most obvious example being to reverse the alphabet, so that *z* stands for *a* and *y* for *b*, etc. Such a transposition cipher would read:

Alphabet of plain text	abcdefghijklmnopqrstuvwxyz
Alphabet of cipher	zyxwvutsrqponmlkjihgfedcba

and *Washington* would be spelled *dzhsrmtglm.*

Perhaps the cleverest transposition cipher ever devised—it is so good that the British Army uses it in the field and, moreover, has published text books about it—is the very simple "Playfair" cipher. First a square is drawn, divided into fifths each way. This arrangement gives twenty-five spaces, to contain the letters of the alphabet—*I* and *J* being put in one square because there would never be any plain sentence in which it would not be quite obvious which one of them is needed to complete a word of which the other letters are known.

Next a "key word" is chosen—and herein lie the cleverness and the simplicity of this cipher, because every time the key word is changed, the whole pattern of the alphabet is changed. Suppose the key word is *Gardenia*. It is now spelled out in the squares:

The second A is left out, as there must not, of course, be duplicates on the keyboard. Now the rest of the alphabet is written into the squares in their regular sequence:

That is the complete keyboard. The method for using it is this:

The message is written out in plain text; for example:

DESTROY BRIDGE AT ONCE

(Only capital letters are commonly used in cipher work.) This message is now divided into groups of two letters, in the same order, so that it reads:

DE ST RO YB RI DG EA TO NC EX

(The X is added to complete the group and is called a *null.*) These groups of twos are now ciphered from the keyboard into other groups of twos, by the following method:

Where two joined letters of the original message appear in the same *horizontal* row on the keyboard, the next letter to the right is substituted for each. Thus, the first two letters of our message are DE. They occur in the same horizontal row on our keyboard. Consequently, for D we write E, and for E we go "on around the world" to the right, or back to the other end of the row, and write G for E. This gives us DE enciphered as EG.

Where two joined letters of the original message appear in the same *vertical* row on the keyboard, the next letter below is substituted for each.

Where two joined letters of the original message appear neither in the same horizontal nor the same vertical row on the keyboard, we imagine a rectangle with the two letters at the opposite corners, and in each case substitute the letter found on the keyboard at the other corner of the same horizontal row. This looks complicated, but in reality is very simple. For example, take the third two-letter group of our message—RO. The rectangle in this case is

R D E
B C F
L M O

and for R we substitute E, and for O we substitute L.

Substituting our whole message by this system, it reads:

Original	DE	ST	RO	YB	RI	DG	EA	TO	NC	EX
Cipher	EG	TU	EL	XC	AB	EA	GR	UM	IF	RZ

As telegraph operators are accustomed to send these gibberish messages in groups of five letters (so that they can check errors, knowing that when only four appear in a group, for example, something has been left out) these enciphered groups of twos are now combined into groups of fives, so that the finished cipher reads:

EGTUE LXCAB EAGRU MIFRZ

The foregoing looks extremely complicated, but the truth is that anybody, after half an hour's practice, can put a message into this kind of cipher ("Playfair" cipher) almost as fast as he can print the straight English of it in capital letters. And unless the person who reads it knows the key word which determined the pattern on his keyboard, he would have to be an expert to decipher it, and even he could do it only after a good deal of work.

Another ingenious cipher is called the "Chess Board." First, a sheet of paper is ruled into squares exactly like a chess board—that is, a square divided into eighths each way. This arrangement gives, of course, sixty-four small squares. Then, by agreement between the people who intend to use this cipher, sixteen of these squares are agreed upon and are cut out of the sheet with a knife. Suppose, for example, this pattern is chosen:

and the squares showing in white are cut out.

Next, another sheet of paper is ruled into a chess board, of exactly the same size as the first. The perforated sheet is now laid on top of the second sheet, so that the squares on the one exactly cover the squares on the other. Now, with a pen or pencil, the plain text of the secret message is printed on the under sheet by writing through the perforations of the upper sheet, only one letter being written in each square. This, of course, permits the writing of sixteen letters of the message.

Suppose the complete message is to be:

"Authorize payment ten million dollars to buy copper for shipment to Germany." Then the lower sheet, after we have written through the perforations, will look like this:

The perforated sheet is now turned to the right through one fourth of a complete revolution, so that the top of it is at the right side of the lower sheet and so that the two chess boards again "match up." This operation exposes, through the perforations, a new set of sixteen open squares on the lower sheet. The writing of the message is continued...

Again the perforated sheet is turned to the right, and sixteen more letters are written. Once more, and the whole sixty-four squares are utilized, looking like the last cut on the previous page.

These letters are now put upright, like this.

They are now read from left to right and from the first line down, like ordinary reading matter. They are then grouped into fives for telegraphic transmission, and an *X* added at the end to make an even five-group there. Thus the message, as transmitted, reads:

SADUL RRYAL TOHOF TRLNO IRNEI
MZNPI EEIPE PGOMC APYTU LAYHM
EBOOM NRNOT TESTX

When this message is received, it can, of course, be quickly deciphered by printing it out on a chess board and placing over it a sheet perforated according to the prearranged pattern.

This survey of codes and ciphers does not more than scratch the surface of the subject, nor more than suggest the almost infinite variations that are possible—in ciphers especially. It simply gives a groundwork for an understanding of the German secret messages now to be described.

Among the most interesting of these secret messages is the series of wireless telegrams by means of which the German money was paid to Bolo Pasha for the purchase of the Paris *Journal*—one of the principal episodes in the treasonable intrigue for which Bolo was recently executed by a French firing squad. These messages were in English, and meant exactly what they said, except for the proper names and the figures, which were *code*. To decode them, it was necessary only to make the following substitutions:

William Foxley = Foreign Office
Charles Gledhill = Count Bernstorff
Fred Hooven = Guaranty Trust Company (New York)
$500 = $500,000

and to all other figures add three ciphers to arrive at the real amount. For example, one of these messages read: "Paid Charles Gledhill five hundred dollars through Fred Hooven." This meant: "Paid Count Bernstorff five hundred *thousand* dollars through Guaranty Trust Company."

The story of these messages is briefly this: Marie Paul Bolo started life as a barber, became an adventurer and, in the service of the Khedive of Egypt, received the title of Pasha for a financial service which he rendered him. Returning to France as Bolo Pasha, he married two wealthy women and lived in grand style on their money. He became an intimate of Charles Humbert, another adventurer, who achieved political power by questionable methods and became a member of the French Senate. In the meantime, the Khedive had been deposed by the British on account of his pro-Turkish (and hence pro-German) activities after the Great War began. Abbas Hilmi joined the colony of ex-rulers in Switzerland, and there became a part of the German system of intrigue. He received money from the Germans and, after he had deducted his "squeeze" (which sometimes amounted to half the total), he paid over the rest to Bolo, to be used by Bolo, Humbert, and ex-Premier Caillaux in an effort to restore Caillaux to power and then to further the propaganda for an early and hence inconclusive peace.

Either this method of supplying the French traitors with funds became too dangerous, or the Germans preferred to keep their gold and wished to use their credit in the United States to get American gold for this purpose. In any event, Bolo Pasha appeared in New York early in March, 1916. Strangely enough, this French citizen bore letters of introduction to several Germans. The most important was addressed to Adolf Pavenstedt, who was senior partner in G. Amsinck & Company and for many years a chief paymaster of the German spy system in this country. Through Pavenstedt,

Bolo met Hugo Schmidt, a director of the Deutsche Bank of Berlin, a government institution, who had been sent to this country soon after the war broke out to provide complete coöperation between the older representatives of the Deutsche Bank here and the management in Berlin.

Through Pavenstedt, as messenger, Bolo also got in touch with Bernstorff, and arranged the details of the plan by which Bolo was to receive 10 million francs from the German Government. He was to use this money to buy the Paris *Journal*, which would then be edited by Senator Humbert, who agreed to change its editorial policy to favour an immediate peace. As the *Journal* is one of the most powerful dailies in France, with a circulation among more than a million and a half readers, the sinister possibilities of this scheme are readily seen.

MR. A. BRUCE BIELASKI

Who, as Chief of the Bureau of Investigation of the Department of Justice, organized and managed the Government agents who unraveled the German plots and captured the plotters.

Bernstorff committed the financial details to Hugo Schmidt. He, in turn, asked Berlin by wireless for suitable credits in American banking houses. These were arranged with the Guaranty Trust Company and the National Park Bank—for many years American correspondents of the Deutsche Bank. The amounts were then credited to G. Amsinck & Company, of which Pavenstedt had long been senior partner. He, in turn, placed them, with the New York branch of the Royal Bank of Canada, to the account of Bolo Pasha. As the exchange rate at the time ran in favour of American dollars and against French francs, the 10 million francs (normally equal to about 2 million dollars) which Bolo got, required only $1,683,500 of American money—which is just the sum of the amounts named in the wireless messages.

The *Journal* was actually bought by Bolo and Humbert, but before they could do much damage with it, they were arrested, and Bolo has already been executed.

The Hindus in this country, who were plotting with the Germans the revolution that should destroy the British rule in India, used two systems for their secret messages. The first was this *substitution cipher*:

The message, "Leave San Francisco" would be written, in this cipher, as follows:

25 15 11 41 15 35 11 27 16 34 11 27 13 22 35 13 31

by giving each letter of the message the number to the left of it, combined with the number above it.

The other system used by the Hindus was a *book code*. They agreed upon a small English dictionary of a certain edition, and wrote from it messages that were also groups of numbers, after this fashion: 625–2–11 27–1–36 45–2–20 and so on. The first figure in each group was the number of the page on which the word would be found, the second figure gave the column, and the third figure was the number of the word in the column, counting from the top of the page.

But perhaps the most dramatic of all the intercepted messages (except the Luxburg and Zimmerman notes, of which the story cannot yet be told) were those which revealed the part played by well-known Irish-American leaders in the ill-fated Casement revolution in Ireland. The story of the Casement expedition is too familiar to need to be retold. And comment upon the political morals of Justice Cohalan and John Devoy becomes superfluous in the light of these messages. American citizens (one of them signally honoured with public office in New York), both held their Irish blood superior, in their duty of loyalty, to the United States, using their citizenship as a cloak under which to strike at Great Britain, which has been for a quarter century the chief bulwark of this country against Germany's plan to conquer us and to impose upon our country the most hateful tyranny in the history of the world.

CHAPTER VIII
The Tiger of Berlin Meets the Wolf of Wall Street

Franz Von Rintelen was the German tiger who missed his spring. He was the most powerful, the most dangerous, agent of the Kaiser in the United States: and to-day he nurses his hatred of us behind prison bars. But he did not retire to confinement until after our Government completed an extremely difficult and tedious investigation that was made necessary by his care in concealing the insidious work of propaganda and destruction in which he had engaged.

Rintelen was a tiger in the implacable hatred he bore this country and in the ferocity with which he carried that hatred into action. Sent to America in 1915 to hinder the shipment of munitions to the Allies, he sought first to poison the press, then to corrupt labour, and, not content with these things, he finally tried to hire thugs to burn, to dynamite, and to assassinate, where other persuasions failed; and he did succeed in setting fire to thirty-six ships at sea, causing millions of dollars of loss, and imperiling hundreds of human lives.

Rintelen had, however, the other side of the tiger's character—its graces. When the —— made port at New York on April 3, 1915, it bore as passenger one Émil Gasché, a Swiss. The moment Gasché passed the customs officers Gasché ceased to exist, and in his place appeared handsome young Von Rintelen, unexpectedly arrived in America for his fourth visit and renewing pleasant acquaintanceships in society and in Wall Street. He was "the same old chap," to quote his own description of himself in one of his letters—rich, of a family long accustomed to riches; well-bred, of a family long proud of its aristocratic connection with the Imperial Court at Berlin (his father had long been the equivalent of our Secretary of the Treasury); young, the youngest of the chief bankers of Germany; handsome, with the good looks that come of regular features and of a slender frame hardened by athletics and made distinguished by the bearing of an officer; a sportsman, who raced his yacht in the Emperor's regattas at Kiel—an affable, cultivated, witty, accomplished man of the world. No wonder he had been popular on his former visits. On one of them he had opened in New York a branch of the Deutsche Bank, one of the greatest of the government-controlled banks of Germany, and on another he had widened these financial relationships with Wall Street. He had travelled the country over and knew people everywhere; and he knew about hundreds more, even to their private affairs in money and politics and those intimate weaknesses that pass into the gossip of the smoking-room. He spoke the language with only the slightest accent but in its purest form, and was adept in our peculiar kind of humour—altogether, a fine and likable fellow, who liked us.

Until the war. And until the Germans, stung by the lost illusions of a quick and glorious victory, facing the gray outlook of a long and bitter struggle, looking about for some one to blame for their plight, and wearied of "strafing" England, found a new narcotic in a hatred of America. America, that made the cartridges and shells that patched up the unpreparedness of France and Britain and Russia, which Germany had calculated as one of the factors in the equation of victory. America, that—as their rising rage made their voices shriller—"is murdering our sons and brothers on every battlefield from Switzerland to the sea for the sake of blood-bought gold."

This cry became an article of fanatical faith to the German people. It became likewise a very practical problem to the hard-headed leaders in Berlin. If they could cut off this supply of munitions, the Allies could be beaten. There was no hope of cutting it off at sea—the British Navy would attend to that. It must be stopped at its source: stopped in America, by a made-to-order public opinion, or by corruption, or by violence—but stopped.

"Whom shall we send to America?" was their problem. Rintelen was chosen. He could be trusted—he was a director of the Deutsche Bank, he knew America. He was given credit at the Hamburg-American Line office in New York for $547,000, authority for as many millions more as he wanted, independent powers as great as the German Ambassador's at

Washington, the instructions of the German Government, and the blessing of the Fatherland.

An American traitor in Berlin gave Rintelen his cue for operations in America. This man's name is known, and will one day be written alongside Benedict Arnold's, but to disclose it now would interfere with more practical efforts for his mortal punishment. Part of that punishment he is already enduring—he is still in Germany. This traitor told Rintelen that the most useful man in America for his purpose was David Lamar, of New York. Rintelen fixed that name in his memory, and left Berlin.

His first barrier was the old, old barrier to German conquest, the British blockade. Rintelen ran that under cover of the Swiss passport, under the name of Gasché.

Arrived in New York on April 3d, Rintelen lost no time in getting acquainted with Lamar. He disclosed to him his mission to this country and the money he had to execute it. The Tiger of Berlin met the Wolf of Wall Street.

And how the Wolf's eyes must have glistened, for he was at the leanest of the hungry days which regularly followed seasons of opulence in the ups and downs which varied the career of this extraordinary man. For Lamar was, and is, an extraordinary man. Endowed by nature with a fascinating personality and with a brilliant mind, which he had enriched by study, a man capable of great things, he was possessed by that strange perversity which often afflicts men of exceptional cleverness—he would rather make one dollar by adroit crookedness than a million by unexciting honesty. Perhaps his origin affected his character—he declined, on the witness stand, to give his true name and parentage on the ground that to do so would bring disgrace upon persons still living. He entered Wall Street as a young man from nowhere, and at first gave promise of a brilliant and honourable career. He early made his mark in finance. He was employed by J. P. Morgan & Company and other great banking concerns, and in those days of his legitimate activities amassed a large fortune. But this was dissipated in gambling on the stock market, and then Lamar gravitated to the gutter. For years it was a by-word on the Street that if you wanted a clever man to do a crooked job, David Lamar was the man you were looking for. He had the brains to do it right, he had the presence to "get away with it," and he would do anything for money.

These traits had got him into trouble shortly before Rintelen met him. When the Pujo Committee of Congress was investigating the "money trust" several years ago, some crooked brokers in Wall Street wanted some inside information that was going to affect the price of certain stocks in which they were interested. They could not get this information by legitimate means, and so they adopted Lamarian means. Lamar knew that a member of Congress was entitled to ask for this information. Mr. Mitchell Palmer was a Member of Congress. Lamar had one of his devious inspirations. He called up a banker's office, got the man there who knew what Lamar wanted to know, declared that he was Mr. Palmer, and demanded the information—and got it. Lamar repeated the exploit several times. But once too often. He was detected, arrested and tried, convicted, and on December 3, 1914, was sentenced to two years' imprisonment for the crime of impersonating an officer of the Government. He appealed the case on the ground that a Representative in Congress was not "an officer of the Government." When Rintelen met him the following April, Lamar was out on bail pending the decision on this appeal.

Lamar was then in desperate straits. Bad luck had followed him in the Street for two years, and had crowned his misfortunes with this expensive trial and threatened imprisonment. He owed money everywhere for personal expenses; the merchants with whom he traded had stopped his credit; he had descended to borrowing from his friends in sums as small as two dollars at a time. Then he met Rintelen, who was on fire with a passion that blinded him to consequences and who flourished before the eyes of the famished Wolf a half million dollars of real money. Here was manna fallen from heaven.

"Could Lamar help Rintelen!" With his most convincing eloquence, Lamar assured him that he could. Never had Rintelen been better advised, so Lamar declared to him, than when his friend in Berlin had given him his name. For he had friends in Washington, he whispered, men powerful in the Government. And friends among the labouring people, the men whose hands made those munitions Rintelen had come to stop, and whose hands might be paralyzed by the clever use of brains and money. Lamar would supply the brains: Rintelen would supply the money. The Wolf saw good hunting ahead.

Lamar laid before Rintelen a scheme. They would capitalize the American passion for peace: they would capitalize in particular the labouring man's aversion to war. A section of opinion among labouring men held that wars were instigated by capitalists for gain, and were fought by labouring men who gave their lives to make good the selfish ambitions of the rich. And one of the American people's deepest convictions was that war was an odious moral crime; and that universal peace was attainable by the pursuit of moral ideals.

Lamar declared, then, that by working through his friends in labour, he could organize the workers of America so that they would refuse to work on the implements of destruction of "capitalistic" war. And that, by working through his friends in the Government, he could create a national sentiment that would force Congress to place an embargo on munitions. But these things would cost money. Lamar never forgot money.

Now we see a sudden transformation in Lamar's circumstances. The frayed debtor appeared in his old haunts garbed in the most fastidious selections of the tailor; the accumulated debts of years were paid; the subway and the street car gave way to automobiles—and Lamar was particular that the garage should supply only the fine car that was father to the Liberty motor. He moved his family from a cheap apartment in New York to a fine house at Pittsfield, Mass. His own quarters were the hotels Astor and Belmont in New York, the Willard in Washington, the La Salle in Chicago, the Claypool in Indianapolis. Things were looking up.

Lamar carried other men with him on his rising tide of fortune. Frank Buchanan, labour Representative in Congress from the Seventh District of Illinois (North Chicago), likewise became a traveller and the patron of exclusive hotels. Henry B. Martin, who eked out a precarious living in the lobbies of Congress, after a dubious career as an officer of the Knights of Labour in the 'nineties, framed his wizened figure in a new and luxurious setting. H. Robert Fowler, the splendid high light of whose gray life as a half-lawyer, half-farmer, in a country town in Illinois, was expiring in the last days of a term in Congress, was suddenly revived, before his final extinguishment, by the light glittering from anonymous gold. Herman J. Schulteis, whose talents, insufficient for success in the law, had been more profitably employed in the defunct Anti-Trust League (of which more later), rose rapidly in the monetary scale.

These men were the instruments Lamar used in his scheme to stop the munitions industry and to get Rintelen's money. That scheme was to build up a great political organization of labouring men and farmers. This organization would oppose the making and shipment of munitions; it would exert pressure to compel workers to abandon the factories, and it would exert pressure to compel Congress to declare an embargo on the shipment of arms. This organization was labelled "Labour's National Peace Council."

Lamar, fortified with Rintelen's money, launched his scheme in Washington. This scheme was an inspiration of genius. Able lawyers have declared that no cleverer conspiracy has ever come to their attention. Its beauty was its simplicity. Rintelen dealt with no one but Lamar—the other leaders never saw him, and most of them never heard of him until after the scheme was exposed by the Government. In his turn, Lamar operated entirely through Martin. To Martin he gave his instructions to see labour leaders, to organize the fake Peace Council, to hold its camouflage "convention," to flood the country with lecturers and printed matter urging an embargo on munitions. And through Martin he paid the bills.

Lamar and Martin were old associates. They had worked together in the Anti-Trust League, another of the creations of Lamar's restless mind. The Anti-Trust League originated in the feverish 'nineties, when the country had its fears that the growth of great corporations spelled the control of the Government by monopolies. The League had its days of prominence when it was financed by big interests that used it to fight other big interests to get the things they both wanted. But in 1915 the League was a skeleton, consisting of Lamar, Martin, Schulteis, and a few others, held together by the bond of small salaries drawn from some source that preferred to remain unknown.

When Martin undertook to organize Labour's National Peace Council, under the direction of Lamar, the first man he approached was Frank Buchanan. Buchanan was labour's leading champion on the floor of Congress. He had been president of the international union of the structural iron workers, and he had earned the confidence of organized labour, and the friendship of Samuel Gompers, the patriarch of organized labour.

Lamar, Buchanan, and Martin, assisted by Fowler and Schulteis, engineered a mass meeting of workingmen in Chicago in June, 1915, at which resolutions were adopted calling for a convention of labourers and farmers at Washington to protest against the traffic in munitions. The same men, with this "mandate" behind them, met in Washington on June 22d, and organized Labour's National Peace Council. They prepared printed appeals, in the high language of humanitarianism, addressed to the labour unions and the granges, and mailed them by the ton to all parts of the country. They offered to pay all travelling expenses and for lost time to delegates which these bodies should send to a convention to be held in Washington on July 31st and August 1st.

As a preliminary to this convention, Martin paid labour leaders and other speakers to go into all sections of the United States and address labour unions and granges. Probably all these speakers acted in good faith. They were pacifists, and when they got an opportunity to preach their doctrine, they accepted it. The opportunity seemed legitimate enough—the name of Frank Buchanan as a sponsor of the movement was sufficient. Their audiences, too, were sincere. Workmen and farmers had before their eyes the contrast of their own peaceful land with a Europe drenched in blood. The blessings of peace were never more apparent. They sent delegates gladly to a meeting that seemed designed to perpetuate those blessings.

But Samuel Gompers opposed the convention of Labour's National Peace Council. He, too, was a pacifist—had for years taken a leading part in the movement for international peace. But Gompers was a thoughtful man as well. And experienced. And wise. He told Buchanan some things Buchanan should have told himself. Buchanan came from Chicago to Atlantic City to meet Mr. Gompers and upbraid him for his opposition to the Council. Mr. Gompers gave him some fatherly advice. In effect, he said:

"Frank, you have earned a good name in labour. We are proud of you, and we trust you. You are at life's meridian, with years of useful service ahead. But listen to an old man, who sees the shadows growing very long, and who has watched many movements come and go. You are in wrong. This scheme is bad. There is too much easy money being passed around in it. Labour hasn't got money to spend like this. Somebody who has not labour's interests at heart is putting up that money.

"And take the Council's aims themselves. Suppose you succeed in stopping the manufacture of munitions—what will happen to labour? Two years ago, our boys were walking the streets, begging for a job. To-day, every man of them has work, and wages are going up. War work has done that. Do you want to stop the opportunity of labour to make a living?"

But Gompers's eloquence left Buchanan cold. In the face of his pleadings and advice, Buchanan accepted $2,700 from Martin in the following six weeks. He saved his face at the last minute by resigning the presidency of Labour's National Peace Council the day before the convention met.

The convention met in Washington on July 31st, at the New Willard Hotel. Its members were impressed, as it was intended that they and the country in general should be impressed, by the sonorous voice and important presence of Hannis Taylor, former American Minister to Spain and author of text books on constitutional and international law, such as "The Origin and Growth of the English Constitution" and "International Public Law." He made an opening address in which, from his heights of knowledge, he solemnly declared that munitions shipments were in violation of international law. His address was largely devoted to assurances to his hearers that he was an authority on such matters and that they could take his opinion as disposing of the legal aspect of this question. Mr. Taylor was there to lend distinction to the gathering, and he left no doubts in their minds that he thought he was doing it.

But when the delegates got down to business, there was trouble. The farmer delegates became suspicious—they had vague fears of the source of the money that was paying the bills; they did not like the company they found themselves in. They first declined to bind their constituents to the resolutions that were offered: then they left the convention.

On the second day, the labour delegates became equally restless. Buchanan had withdrawn. The delegates who used the opportunity of being in Washington to call on Mr. Gompers came away from his office with heavy hearts. Returning to the Willard, they saw the machinery being manipulated by the discredited Martin and Schulteis. "What have these fellows got to do with us?" they asked one another. And then they asked "these fellows" quite bluntly, "Who's putting up the money for this show?" Martin, backed to the wall of the Willard bar by their insistent demand for an answer, replied with an evasive, "What difference does it make?" And when they shouted that it made a profane lot of difference, he answered defiantly that it was all right "even if it's German money."

That finished the labour delegates. They, too, went home.

But the ringleaders had put out a resounding resolution calling for an embargo on munitions. And though the convention had fizzed out, it had done an enormous lot of harm. Thousands of labouring men and farmers had been indoctrinated with a specious pacifism that was reflected later in the attempts to evade the Conscription Act when we entered the war. The Government to-day is contending with the moral antagonisms aroused in certain sections of the country by the orators and writers of Labour's National Peace Council.

In this moral infection, the work of Hannis Taylor played an important part. He wrote legal opinions for the Council, declaring that the traffic in munitions was unconstitutional. He received $700 for this work. These opinions were printed and distributed broadcast, and did much harm. More recently, Taylor was counsel for Robert Cox, the Missouri draft registrant who sued to restrain General Leonard Wood from sending him with his regiment to France. On his behalf, Hannis Taylor contended that the Conscription Act was unconstitutional, asserting that the only power of Congress to call out troops was under the militia clause of the Constitution which reads: "To execute the laws of the Union, suppress insurrections and repel invasions." This meant, so Taylor contended, that no citizen could be sent, against his will, outside the United States to fight its battles.

This absurd doctrine, which would force us to fight this war on our own soil instead of allowing us to defend ourselves in Europe against German aggression, was promptly punctured by the Supreme Court of the United States. In his brief before that Court Hannis Taylor used language so violent that the counsel for the Government asked that it be expunged from the record. Taylor in his brief accused the President of being a "dictator," of seizing powers "in open defiance of the judgments" of the Supreme Court, and of demanding "such an aggregation of powers as no monarch ever wielded in any constitutional government that ever existed."

The decision of the Supreme Court, affirming the Government's right to draft its citizens for service overseas, was delivered by Chief Justice White. That stern old veteran of the Lost Cause in our Civil War, speaking with the aloofness and dignity of that august Court, in measured terms expressed an opinion of Mr. Hannis Taylor that is worth repeating. He said:

... we must notice a suggestion made by the Government that because of impertinent and scandalous passages contained in the brief of the appellant the brief should be stricken from the files. Considering the passages referred to and making every allowance for intensity of zeal and an extreme of earnestness on the part of counsel, we are nevertheless constrained to the conclusion that the passages justify the terms of censure by which they are characterized in the suggestion made by the Government. But despite this conclusion which we regretfully reach, we see no useful purpose to be subserved by granting the motion to strike. On the contrary, we think the passages on their face are so obviously intemperate and so patently unwarranted that if as a result of permitting the passages to remain on the files they should come under future observation, they would but serve to indicate to what intemperance of statement an absence of self-restraint or forgetfulness of decorum will lead and therefore admonish of the duty to be sedulous to obey and respect the limitations which an adhesion to them must exact.

In all the operations of Labour's National Peace Council, including its convention, Lamar kept in the background, as he knew labour had no reason to own him or to love him. Buchanan and the rest supplied the proper colour of propriety. From his retreat in the Willard Hotel in Washington, Lamar was sending ecstatic telegrams, reporting progress, signing the name of David H. Lewis, and receiving in reply approving messages from Rintelen, who used Jones, Miller, and Muller as aliases. The convention seemed a great success. And its preparation and operation had got the German's money. Of the $547,000 that Rintelen brought, Lamar got more than $300,000. It looked so good to Rintelen that he was ready to get more—from Germany or from his limitless sources of credit here.

But all was not well with Rintelen. He had other lines out besides Lamar's, and he caught some disquieting fish—some of which he did not identify until later. First, he was playing the social game not wisely but too well. He gave dinner parties; was a guest at others. He should have been more politic than he was. The *Lusitania* was sunk on May 7th. Instead of adopting the manner of a man deep enough in intrigue to know that he should speak of this crime as a lamentable blunder of his country's, he justified it. His words gave the gravest offense to his guests. He went further, and threw out hinted threats of other perils that would confront ships carrying munitions—hints that he himself had had a hand in the mysterious fires on ships that were almost a daily occurrence. Some dinner guests in New York took him seriously and reported him to the

Government, which had been suspicious of him almost from the day of his arrival in this country.

Also, Rintelen undertook to get newspaper publicity favourable to an embargo on the shipment of munitions. He got himself introduced to "Jack" Hammond, an old newspaper man in New York, and closed with him a contract for syndicate articles in a chain of papers across the country. He met Hammond as one Fred Hansen, a ship captain. (Hammond later testified that Rintelen told him that he "killed" Hansen the day after the *Lusitania* was sunk.) After sizing Hammond up as worthy of trust, he re-introduced himself as E. V. Gibbons, a purchasing agent, with offices in the building occupied in part by the Transatlantic Trust Company. And at length he confided to Hammond his real importance in the scheme of things German.

Early in this relationship Hammond became sure that this man was planning to violate the laws of the United States, and he reported the matter to the Department of Justice. The Department, already suspicious, asked Hammond to keep up his connection with Rintelen, and through this means it learned a great deal about him. Not enough to cause his arrest—Rintelen never confided that much in any American but Lamar, who had his own reasons for silence.

Out of Rintelen's multifarious activities arose many of the mysterious fires and explosions in munitions plants, the burning of ships at sea, the attempts on the Welland Canal in Canada, strikes in war industries, and the like. The discovery of Dr. Walter A. Scheele's part in the incendiary bombs matter, and his connection with Rintelen, began to make the ground fairly warm under Rintelen's feet. And the Government was taking an uncomfortable interest in Labour's National Peace Council. Rintelen became uneasy.

His fears were now fed from a new quarter. Andrew D. Meloy became a confidant of his, and Meloy had his own axe to grind. Rintelen had taken an interest in the German activities in Mexico, and almost from the day of his arrival had been intimate in this work with Federico Stallforth, a German banker of Mexico City who joined Rintelen in New York. Stallforth had offices with Meloy at 55 Liberty Street, and when the Transatlantic Trust Company became embarrassed by Rintelen's presence, Stallforth persuaded Meloy to rent Rintelen desk room. Their acquaintance started there, about July 1st.

Meloy was a well-known engineer and promoter. He had exploited concessions in Mexico—railroad rights of way and gold mines—and in his home state of New Jersey had floated some real-estate "developments." Meloy saw in Rintelen exactly what Lamar had seen—a lot of real money and an eagerness too great for caution. He began to belittle Lamar's scheme. Labour's National Peace Council would never do. It looked good on paper, but it would never stop the shipment of munitions. He even hinted that Lamar had been "playing" Rintelen. Now, if Rintelen wanted a real scheme, certain to succeed, he knew the very thing. Direct action—stop the bluffing and the dangerous intrigues. Buy the whole munitions output of the country. Bid high enough to get it, pay for it outright, and store it. That would cost money, lots of it: but what was money in comparison with the certainty of German victory which this plan would insure?

Rintelen was dazzled. Here was the authentic voice of American big business speaking. A magnificent scheme. He would take it to Germany, take Meloy with him, and get his Government to O. K. it.

But how get back to Germany? He had grave doubts about the Gasché passport being good again. He put the question to Meloy, and Meloy advised against it. There was a better way: get a new passport under a new name. So for a few days Rintelen became "Edward V. Gates, wine merchant, of Millersburg, Pa." In this guise Meloy introduced him to one of his own real-estate salesmen, and Rintelen took this man to dinner once or twice to work up the illusion. Then, one day, he asked the salesman to go with him to the passport bureau in New York and be his witness to an application for a passport. The salesman went, and in good faith swore that Rintelen was Edward V. Gates. His faith was not so good when he swore he had known him for three years. The application was transmitted telegraphically to Washington. Much to Rintelen's astonishment and alarm, it was denied.

Meanwhile, Meloy had been working on a devious scheme to protect himself in his mission to Berlin. He must be cloaked in eminent respectability on this errand, for it would be an unpopular one with the British if they knew its real purpose, and he must hide that. First of all, he would take his wife, who did not know what his mission was. She had taken an active interest before the war in the peace movements centring at The Hague, and nothing was more natural than that she should wish now, during the war, to renew her friendships in Holland with an eye to furthering a cause now more than ever vital to the world.

But Meloy was not content with only one companion. He must have others who would expand the picture of innocence abroad. One of his neighbours in the suburb on the Jersey Coast where he made his country home was a wealthy woman known widely in America for her interest both in the peace and suffrage movements. Meloy telephoned to her and asked her to see him at his home. This lady drove over one summer evening in her motor car, accompanied by two women friends. The friends sat in the open car while she sat on the porch talking to Meloy. Meloy is very deaf; the lady had to talk loudly to make him hear. Meloy differed from most deaf people, who usually speak in a lower tone than those who hear well—he went rather to the other extreme, and spoke louder than most folks do. The women in the car heard the conversation, and they heard it a second time when their friend repeated it to them on the way home. And the Government heard it also, from the lips of all three.

The burden of the conversation was this: Meloy was taking his wife to Europe for a vacation; they were going to Holland, where so many forward-looking movements for the good of mankind made their international headquarters; he would be drawn aside a great deal by business affairs and Mrs. Meloy would be lonesome; he was anxious to provide companionship for her, if the lady would accompany them, he would pay all her expenses, he would assure her that her journey would be made *de luxe*, he would (he put it more delicately) even add a money consideration, he would see that the journey included a visit to war-bound Germany, now so difficult of access, that in Germany she should have *entrée* to social circles so exclusive that they were inaccessible even to the American Ambassador, and that, to crown all, she should be presented to the Kaiser.

The lady said she would think it over. It was an attractive invitation, but she did not just like it—perhaps it was too attractive. She talked it over with her friends: they advised against it. She telephoned Meloy next day and declined.

Meloy repeated the invitation to several women. All declined. Then, as the *Noordam* was to sail on August 3d, and he had no more time, he decided to take his secretary, a Miss Brophy.

Rintelen was now thoroughly alarmed. The Government's refusal to grant his fraudulent application for a passport indicated that it knew about him. The Government was getting "warm" in its investigation of the incendiary bombs. The Government was taking an unpleasant interest in Labour's National Peace Council. Rintelen felt irresistibly the pangs of *Heimweh*, the longing for home. He must go, at any risk. He would chance it as Gasché again.

So he sailed on the *Noordam*, with Meloy and party. He bore with him Lamar's urgent appeals for more funds for Labour's National Peace Council, now at the high tide of its success. And he was in the hands of Meloy, who was at the first of his own rainbow of hope of millions with which to buy America's munition output—on commission.

At Falmouth the *Noordam* was detained for fourteen hours. The British took a great interest in the Gasché-Meloy party. Gasché's baggage revealed nothing suspicious, but Gasché was removed to a long residence in an internment camp near London. Meloy was detained for several days. Mrs. Meloy soon appeared to be beyond suspicion. Miss Brophy declared that her baggage contained only personal effects. But at the bottom of her last trunk was found a wallet containing Gasché's papers. These were seized, and Miss Brophy and Mrs. Meloy were allowed to proceed to Holland, where they were later rejoined by Meloy.

The Gasché papers were most interesting. They contained some of Rintelen's letters showing his intimacy with well-known New Yorkers, and letters in which he referred to his "official mission" to the United States that were very important, for they proved what Rintelen steadfastly denied, namely, that he was in this country by orders of the German Government. In one of them to a man in Germany, whom he addressed as "Most Honourable Counsellor," he wrote: "Your letter of the 25th March [1915] was sent after me when I was *on an official journey*, and I request you to excuse the delaying in replying." And another letter, from the National Bank Für Deutschland, dated Berlin, 25th May, 1915, and addressed "To the Landed Proprietor, Von Preskow," contained this sentence: "Director Rintelen, who looked after Major Von Katte's account, entered the navy on the outbreak of hostilities, and as he is at present *on an official journey* is not available at the moment."

With Rintelen's internment ended Lamar's golden fortune and Meloy's golden vision and Rintelen's dream of destruction. And now began one of the most difficult and one of the longest tasks of the Department of Justice. For, out of the fragments of evidence at its command, and out of the seemingly innocent public acts of Labour's National Peace Council, and out of the obscure and isolated outrages to ships and factories in the United States, the Department of Justice had to construct a pattern that should prove, by tangible legal evidence, the guilt of Rintelen and Lamar in a plot to violate the laws of the United States.

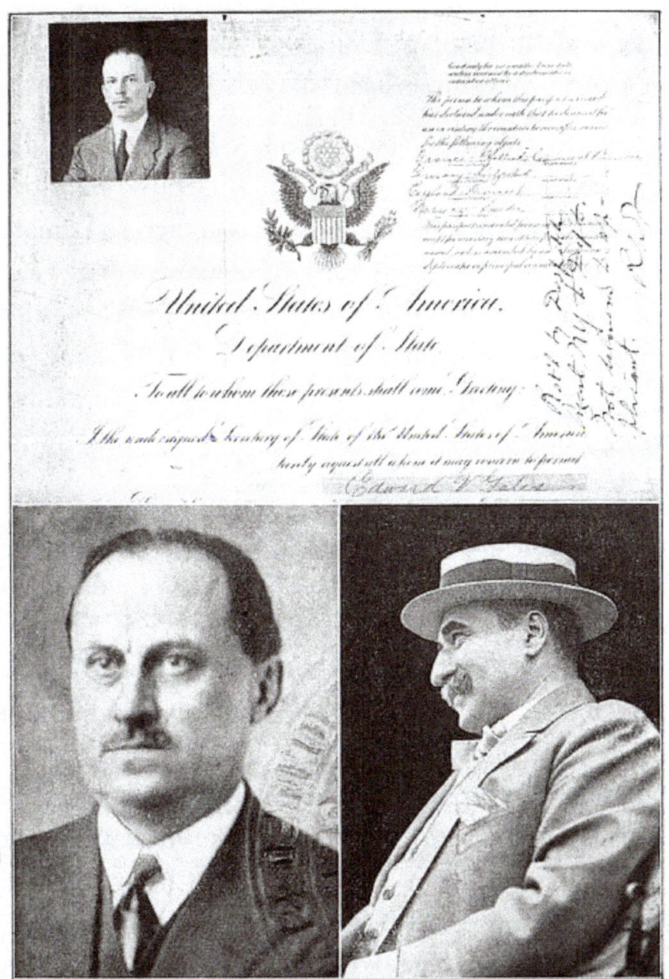

RINTELEN AND HIS CONFEDERATES

Above, Rintelen's photograph on a false passport with which he tried to escape from the United States; left, Andrew D. Meloy; right, David Lamar, "the Wolf of Wall Street"

This long investigation was a fascinating study in human nature. If only Lamar had been a little different in his manners, he might have escaped the clutches of the law. If Rintelen had been as wise as he was clever, he might still be in an internment camp instead of a prison.

Lamar, it may be recalled, had a weakness for automobiles. He hired them on all occasions. They were especially useful to him for conferences with Rintelen. They did not wish to be seen together, so Lamar would drive to an unfrequented spot in Central Park. Rintelen would drive up in another car and get into Lamar's, and then they would go for a long ride while they discussed their plans. Sometimes they would go for hours on the North Shore of Long Island; sometimes for long excursions in the Pelham region of Westchester County, stopping perhaps at a wayside inn and taking a room for greater privacy in their conferences.

An agent of the Department of Justice spent six weeks making the rounds of the garages in New York. He carried Lamar's picture in his pocket. He showed it to every chauffeur in every garage. And every chauffeur who had driven a car for Lamar during that summer of 1915 recognized the picture, and every one of them applied the same epithet to its original that Trampas applied to the Virginian in Owen Wister's book when the Virginian, in response, drew his gun and demanded that "when you call me that, smile!" For Lamar, who was the suave, the gracious, the ultra-polite and charming man to people whom he wished to cajole, was overbearing, fault-finding, and peremptory toward those who served him. His movements in the hotels about the country were several times traced by a rough description completed by a remark about his manner toward servants. No waiter or bell-boy ever forgot him. He was forever "kicking about the service."

This vivid impression that he made on the chauffeurs contributed greatly to his undoing. They remembered him perfectly, and recalled his companions. They recognized Rintelen's photograph. And several of them had overheard parts of the conversations that were useful to the Government. Through these men, Lamar's connection with Rintelen in a conspiracy to violate the Sherman Act by restraining our foreign trade in munitions was established.

One's laundry, too, may be a dangerous thing. Lamar denied that he had stopped at hotels in Chicago and Indianapolis and elsewhere at the same time that Martin and others were there. But handwriting experts proved that the names "David Lenaur," "David Lewis," and the like, on hotel registers on those days were in Lamar's handwriting. And the conclusive proof of their evidence was that the laundry lists of the hotels on those days showed that the laundry mark on the linen of "Lenaur" and of "Lewis" was the laundry mark of Lamar.

Charge accounts at stores may also prove troublesome. It became necessary to find out where Lamar banked his money. That was discovered through Lamar's stomach trouble. He was a patron of a druggist in New York who had his pet prescription for his pet ailment. Lamar sometimes wrote, and sometimes telegraphed, for another bottle of this medicine. A telegram of this kind sent the Government agent to the druggist. Did Lamar ever pay by check? On what banks? The answers led to those banks and thence to others and thence to Lamar's brokers, from one of whom alone evidence was obtained that the whilom bankrupt had lost, in one series of speculations that summer, $38,000 in cash. Whose cash? The Government was able to prove that Lamar had got thousands of dollars from Rintelen, because they produced the men who saw Rintelen pay it, and Lamar was not able to prove that he had got any such sums from anybody else, so the jury took the Government's theory as fact that Lamar was Rintelen's man.

The story of this proof is worth telling. On the witness stand at the trial, George Plockman, the treasurer of the Transatlantic Trust Company (the Austrian bank in New York with which Rintelen kept his funds) described the arrangement Rintelen had made to conceal the passage of money for illegal acts. He had instructed the Transatlantic Trust Company, when it received checks drawn by him in a certain form, to cash them without questioning the identity of the bearer and without requiring him to endorse them.

One check of this kind was presented at the bank one day, and the paying teller brought it to Plockman to ask if he should pay it.

"Who presented it?" asked Plockman.

"That dark man over there," replied the paying teller.

"I thought," said Plockman on the witness stand, "that this man was a Mexican, but while I was looking at him our vice-president came up and when he understood the situation and saw the man he said: 'Mein Gott! Dot is de Volf of Vall Street! I hope Rintelen has not got into *his* clutches!'"

One other incident of the trial should be told. Testimony was brought in that showed how the money for the Peace Council was spent. One item was for funds to pay the expenses of a German preacher from St. Louis to attend the convention at Washington and open the proceedings with prayer. Lamar had never heard of this until he heard it in the courtroom. It was too much for him. When this evidence came out, of the lengths to which his own pupils had out-distanced even their teacher in the art of political camouflage, he burst into roars of uncontrollable laughter which literally stopped all proceedings in court, the tears rolling down his cheeks as he struggled to subdue his mirth.

Out of all the investigations of the Government arose a card index of every man that Rintelen and Lamar had seen during the four months from April 3 to August 3, 1915, of every hotel they had visited, of practically every telephone call they had made and every telegram sent or received, of nearly every dollar they had had and spent. Thousands upon thousands of these cards were made and filed. They convicted both men.

The Government indicted Rintelen, Lamar, Buchanan, Fowler, Martin, Schulteis, and a man named Monnett, for conspiracy to violate the Sherman Act in the operations of Labour's National Peace Council to restrain our foreign trade. Rintelen, Lamar, and Martin were convicted. The rest got the benefit of a very slim doubt, except Frank B. Monnett, the farmer attorney-general of Ohio, whose reputation in the early suit of Ohio to oust the Standard Oil Company from the state had been used as "stage setting" by

Martin. He was freed by the Court before the jury was sent out to deliberate. The convicted men got the limit of the law—one year in jail. Rintelen was likewise indicted for perjury in his application for a passport as Edward V. Gates, and again for another crime against our laws. He was convicted on both charges, and sentenced to several months' imprisonment on each.

No one realized better than the judges who sentenced him how inadequate these punishments to expiate his crimes. But the laws under which Rintelen was convicted—and they were the only laws under which his acts (all committed before our entry into the war) could be questioned—were enacted in times of peace, when no one dreamed of the world conflict or could have imagined how it would affect us when it came.

Rintelen has completed serving time on the first of his three sentences, and has the other two still to serve. The Tiger of Berlin is securely caged, and not likely soon to be again at large.

CHAPTER IX
The American Protective League

On going to war with the great masters of spy craft last year, the United States had only a handful of secret service men to guard its internal frontier. Within our borders were a million and a half men and youths who were enemy aliens. Not all of them hostile, it is true; but all potentially dangerous because great national organizations existed—even shooting societies—through which German influences might reach in a few hours or days. And in every centre of population there were captains and field marshals of German intrigue, supplied with unlimited money, to appeal to their feelings and to lead them should a chance come to strike.

Yet America, during the first year of war, has been singularly peaceful. No serious disturbance has hampered war preparations conducted on a gigantic scale. Even the Selective Service Act, inconsistent with all our volunteer traditions and pride, was accepted almost without opposition. Instead of a red reign of conflagration and civil strife, there have been no outbreaks worthy of the name; and, according to the Underwriters' Association, not a single fire in our munitions plants of a clearly established incendiary character.

Attorney-General Thomas W. Gregory, in fact, had solid grounds for declaring to the executive committee of the American Bar Association recently: "I do not believe that there is to-day any country which is being more capably policed than is the United States." *He added that for every man engaged in detecting and investigating violations of federal laws in April, 1917, there are at least one thousand to-day*; while reports on new cases are coming in at the rate of fifteen hundred a day!

That sounds like a miracle of organization, doesn't it? Even the army, with its pride-compelling record of expansion, is a slow coach beside these legions of "plain-clothes" soldiers who hold our inner lines. Let's see how it happened.

When the war broke, the only secret service work done by the Government was handled by five small organizations. The Department of Justice had its Bureau of Investigation, charged with the discovery of offenses against the federal statutes—not a large force, but quite adequate to its peace-time job. The Treasury Department maintained a secret service with two definite functions—to protect the President's life and person, and to prevent counterfeiting. The Army and Navy had each a few officers detailed to its intelligence service—the gathering of military and naval information and the protection of our own plans and operations. And finally the State Department possessed a small intelligence section of its own. But by comparison with the territory to be covered and the number of active German and Austrian agents in the country, there were few experienced men available for counter-espionage. And there in the background were that million and a half enemy aliens who would bear a lot of watching.

The declaration of war, then, instantly brought an emergency. Part of it the Department of Justice met by striking swift and hard at all who were unquestionably enemy agents. Because of their propaganda and other activities against the Entente Allies, these agents had been under observation for some time. Within forty-eight hours the more dangerous had been rounded up—under the hoary old act of 1798, which gave the President power to intern enemy aliens when their being at liberty might constitute a menace to the public safety.

There remained the urgent need of an immense increase in the Government's counter-espionage forces. It would take thousands of trained and intelligent operatives to keep watch of the German agents and German sympathizers who swarmed throughout the country. As a class, such operatives did not exist: to draft the right kind of raw material from civil life would involve delays, great personal sacrifices on the part of the men drafted, and an enormous yearly budget. Thousands of business and professional careers would be interrupted at critical stages. Most of the men who accepted the call would be risking after-the-war failure in their chosen callings. The work simply couldn't be done that way.

Then it was that the American Protective League found a way to do it.

The League is a volunteer body of 250,000 patriotic Americans, organized with the approval and operating under the direction of the

Department of Justice, Bureau of Investigation. It cross-cuts every commercial, industrial, professional, social, and economic level in American life. Bank presidents and bell hops, judges and janitors, managers and mechanics—all ranks meet on its common platform of loyalty and service. It has woven a net of discreet surveillance across more than a thousand American cities and towns; and the meshes are so small that few active German agents slip through. It reaches out into the country as well. More than 52,000,000 people—about half the population of the United States—live in communities where the League has active and effective organizations; where too, propaganda, or sedition, sabotage or plain slacking are neither popular nor healthy.

The League was born in March, last year, two weeks before we declared war. The idea originated with Mr. A. M. Briggs of Chicago. Mr. Briggs is now Chairman of the National Board of Directors of the American Protective League. He secured authority to establish it as a volunteer auxiliary of the Department of Justice on March 22, 1917. Within a month he had the League in operation with several thousand members. With him, Captain Charles Daniel Frey and Mr. Victor Elting were responsible for its development and the organization of the work. Mr. Frey is organizer and First Chief of the Chicago District, the original working unit of the American Protective League. The plan, the policies, and the methods developed in the Chicago District, which includes 280 cities and towns, were approved by the Department of Justice, and have been generally followed throughout the country as the model and standard for subsequent organizations. Mr. Elting, as Assistant Chief at Chicago, has from the inception of the League been active in the development of its policy. These three, now national directors with headquarters at Washington, are modest about taking any credit for the amazing extension of the League and its extraordinary present usefulness. They insist that the first great response was due to the general recognition of a national crisis, the impulse to do something to meet it, and the patriotic and unselfish coöperation of every local chief and individual operative in the country.

At all events, it was knowledge of how widespread and unscrupulous was the German spy system, and how seriously it was affecting the temper and loyalty of aliens and naturalized citizens, that launched the League. Proposal was made to the Department of Justice that a volunteer auxiliary of simon-pure Americans be formed to keep watch for the Government in every neighbourhood and to make most of the Department's investigations for it. The service would be without pay. No inquiries would be undertaken without reference of the case to the Department first. And no expense accounts would be presented for money spent. Doubts may have existed regarding the feasibility of the plan. Such men as were needed would be hard to interest in the drudgery of police investigation. But Mr. Briggs was confident that there were thousands of business and professional men past service age and necessary to their families and communities who still were fired with patriotism and filled with wrath at the progress of German propaganda and plotting in this country. They were successful men of affairs—men of proved judgment, intelligence, initiative, and energy. The Department could not buy their full time at any price, but it could command their spare time, plus as many work-hours, on occasions, as were necessary to complete any task. There were also men of service age, eager to fight but held at home by obligations or other causes, who would not stint either time or energy in the League's service.

Given authority to go ahead March 22, 1917, the League was organized on military lines. The plan was that each city and its tributary country should be broken up into divisions, in charge of inspectors. Divisions were cut up into districts, with captains in command. And each captain recruited as many working squads, under lieutenants, as the size and character of his district demanded. Reinforcing this territorial organization was another which treated every important industry, trade, and profession, and even large business establishments and office buildings as individual organization units. The territorial organization was known as the Bureau of Investigation; the classified trade, professional, and industrial force as the Bureau of Information. As a matter of fact, they were just the right and left arms of the League. Each had its specialized work to do, but the big jobs in each case were the same.

From the start, the two main functions of the League stood out boldly. The first was "to make prompt and reliable report of all disloyal or enemy activities and of all infractions or evasions of the war code of the United States." The second followed naturally: "to make prompt and thorough investigation of all matters of similar nature referred to it by the Department of Justice." Close coöperation with the local agent of the Department was essential in both instances.

Because the plan had been carefully worked out, the League made a flying start in a great Western city. Inspectors, captains, lieutenants were commissioned and assigned to their units. "Operatives," picked with equal caution, were sworn in and given their credentials. By May first, there were a thousand men engaged in the absorbing new game.

Thousands of investigations taxed the young ardour and endurance of the League—suspected spy activities, seditious speeches, lying reports about the Red Cross, Y. M. C. A., and Knights of Columbus, pro-German propaganda, suspected treasonable conspiracies, sabotage cases and, later, organized and individual efforts to evade the draft. But every member was under pledge to run down to the end any case assigned to him, whether it took a day or a week, and results came speedily.

Though lacking in experience, most of the members had unusual equipment as investigators. Nearly all had imagination and logical, work-trained minds. Many of them were men of means and could devote all of their time to urgent cases. Instead of waiting for an O. K. on a requisition for a motor car, they had machines of their own to use. Without considering how an item would strike a government auditor, they could and did spend their own money to get the facts they sought. Without having to finesse approaches to necessary sources of information, they could usually draw on a wide circle of friends for inside facts which a professional detective might require days to secure.

The League's rule in assigning cases, indeed, is to choose as investigator the man whose social, professional, or business connections are such that he can "clean up" with the least effort and in the shortest space of time. When there are many places to visit, the case goes to a man owning a motor car. If it is complex in character, with lines extending into various industries, clubs, trades, and so on, the work may be divided and several members assigned to it. The main idea is to get the work done, and done quickly—the secondary purpose to make it as easy as may be for the members.

League members knew little about methods of investigation. But they had that priceless gift, intelligence, and they learned by doing. There was such a mass of complaints, tips, and wild guesses concerning enemy activities waiting to be handled, that no extensive schooling could be attempted. The cleverest government operatives available and experienced city and private detectives talked to groups of captains and lieutenants, and these passed along the information to their men. A. Bruce Bielaski, Chief of the Bureau of Investigation, Department of Justice, was quick to recognize the possibilities of the League. Everywhere his organization gave invaluable aid and coöperation in training League members.

Able lawyers made brief but comprehensive digests of the laws involved and the rules of evidence to be observed. Methods of work and problems of authority and conduct were explained at length in a handbook. Supplementing the handbook and the law digest, bulletins were published at intervals to suggest better methods, to report fresh evidence of German plans and propaganda, or to sum up and interpret the new laws which Congress was enacting for the punishment of espionage and sedition.

Close touch was kept at every step with the Department of Justice. Forms for reports and records were adopted, conforming to the system in use by the Department. Carbons of all reports and records were made for the files of the Bureau of Investigation. Eventually a complete record of each case found its way to the master file in Washington. In this way duplication of effort was avoided, complete coöperation assured, and the exact status of any inquiry could be learned in a moment by any one needing the information.

Far from running wild in its enthusiasm to corral all enemy agents, the League tried to give every alien it investigated an American square deal. Perhaps the finest paragraph in the handbook is this one urging the right of aliens to considerate treatment until their unfriendly attitude is revealed:

"Many aliens resident in this country are absolutely loyal to its institutions and its laws, and many individuals having the legal status of alien enemies are not only conducting themselves with due respect to our laws, but are of great value in industry and business. Great care must be exercised by members to avoid unnecessary alarm to aliens and to avoid causing apprehension upon their part as to the fairness and justice of the attitude of the Government toward them. In this regard members will be called upon for the exercise of judgment and discretion of a high order. They should protect citizens and aliens from unjust suspicion, but must fearlessly ascertain and report treason and disloyalty wherever found."

All this has to do with the investigation of specific cases after they have been brought to the League's attention by the report of a member, an outside complaint, or a request from the Department of Justice for an inquiry into the facts. Quite as important in discouraging disloyalty or pro-German activities is the service of League members as eyes and ears for the Government in detecting and making first reports on offenses or intended offenses against the war code of the United States.

This means that every League member is always on the lookout for any word or act that smacks of sedition or espionage. It is here that the classified organization by industries, trades, professions, and individual business establishments develops its full value. When a factory making munitions, clothing, motor trucks, or any other war necessity has been organized as a League unit, the members are on the alert for signs of disturbance. They can quickly report to their supervisor what they have seen or heard, and, after comparing notes, can take precautions against the threatened trouble. If they need outside help in checking up a suspect after working hours, the territorial organization is ready to coöperate. The suspect need never know that he is under suspicion until his guilt or innocence is pretty well established.

Such a factory unit is typical of the League organization in the larger cities. Besides the strictly industrial group, there are usually eight broad divisions, any one of which may be important enough to have an assistant bureau chief, and several captains, lieutenants, and individual units. These divisions take in the real estate, financial, insurance, and professional groups, the hotels, transportation companies, public utilities, and merchandising interests—wholesale, retail, and mail-order. And the industries alone may be numerous and powerful enough to call for separate divisions—munitions, packers' products, food stuffs, war equipment, metal trades, lumber, motor cars, electrical machinery and supplies, chemicals and paints, and so on. It all depends on how numerous and how large are the establishments in each line. Outside the larger cities territorial organization is the rule. When the district is identified with some industry of special value in war, like mining, lumbering, or cattle raising, protection of that industry may be the chief function of the League.

Not only does the classified method of organization help each trade and profession to police itself; it greatly facilitates important inquiries. For example, suppose that the Government wants to find and learn the local errand of a visiting electrical engineer with a German name and considerable cash whom it has had under surveillance elsewhere. On being asked for a report, the League's local Chief assigns the case to one of his deputies. The latter notifies the supervisors of the various hotel units to watch out for the stranger, report his arrival, and keep watch of his letters and telephone calls. He also communicates with the head of the professional division and asks that an electrical engineer be detailed on the case.

When the suspect has been located and the hotel supervisor has transmitted any other information he has been able to get, the engineer member begins work. Going to the hotel he finds or makes a way to become acquainted with the stranger, offers him the usual professional courtesies, and gives him a chance to suggest why he is in town or whom he wants to see. Direct questions are not asked, of course, since they would put the stranger on his guard. After he has carried the inquiry as far as he can, the engineer member quietly and casually goes his way, unless the stranger has accepted his offers of help or hospitality.

If the suspect has "covered up" more than an honest engineer should, he is systematically shadowed by other League operatives during the remainder of his stay. Walking out or staying in his room, travelling in taxicabs or in street cars, making business calls or social calls, one or more of his two "shadows" would probably keep him in sight and make memoranda regarding every person he met and spoke with and every significant circumstance that took place. Only when in a private house or in his hotel room would he escape observation—and even then a fairly close tab would be kept on what he was doing.

A record would be made of every telephone call, every telegram, every letter received, with particular reference to the postmark, dates, and the return cards on the envelopes. His baggage would be inventoried and described, even to its hotel labels, its character, and its probable price and origin. When he finally departed, if the porter bought his tickets for him or whether he purchased them himself at the station, his route, and his first destination—all would be matters of history. One of his "shadows" would even see him safely past the last suburban stop from which he might double back to the city or to a waiting confederate.

This seems a mighty pother to make about an apparently innocent traveller. But the League prefers to work overtime and play safe. The narratives of some of the "tailings" would make marvellous reading if they only led up to the proper dramatic climax. Many of them do—but those are not to be talked about yet awhile. And the others are significant only because they are the records of uninteresting tasks as faithfully executed as though the sheltering doorway or hotel lobby chair were a listening post in France.

Remember that these tasks were made both complex and difficult by the lack of laws defining espionage, disloyalty, and sedition as punishable crimes. That ancient act of 1798 could be invoked for the internment of dangerous enemy aliens. But an American citizen, native or naturalized, could spit treason and plot trouble unchecked so long as he did not run foul of the civil or the criminal code. That is all changed now; the amended Espionage and Sedition Law, signed by the President in June, 1917, is so broad and has such a fine set of serviceable teeth that no disloyal citizen or unfriendly alien can escape the penalty if his guilt can be proved.

For more than a year, however, the League was compelled not only to prove a citizen's pro-German activities; it had also to find a way to punish them, or at least to discourage them. Every inquiry into such a case, therefore, had to be supplemented by an effort to find evidence of an offense against the civil or criminal statutes. And where this failed, a good old-fashioned "talking to" often had the desired effect.

Hatred of "Prussian militarism" and pretended allegiance to the United States were the favourite pose of many propagandists whom the League rounded up and secured billets for in various internment camps. Most of these had taken out their first naturalization papers; except in a few middle and western states like Nebraska, where "first papers" and six months of residence confer the right to vote, this was no protection when evidence of disloyalty or pro-German activity was adduced against them.

Typical of this class was the case of an Austrian officer of reserves who was six months under investigation before he was arrested. Like so many other interned Teutons, his entry into the United States had been by way of the Argentine. Traced back, it was discovered that he had reported to the Austrian Consul in Buenos Aires as an officer of reserves at the first mobilization call, July 27, 1914; and again when he sailed for the United States with a false Swedish passport in 1915. Then, in succession, he had registered at the San Francisco, St. Louis, and Chicago consulates—at the last on September 30, 1915.

In less than six months, however, he had applied for naturalization papers and was arranging to return to Buenos Aires as selling agent for several American houses. When the State Department denied him a passport, he devised another means of keeping watch of American efforts to supplant German houses in the South American markets. This was an export information bureau, but his information was not live enough to hold his clients long. Next he projected a $2,000,000 corporation to take over and operate the German interned steamships at New York. By turns also he was advertising solicitor and automobile salesman.

The occupation he followed always allowed him maximum freedom in moving about and a plausible excuse for approaching almost any one he wanted to reach. Very early in the inquiry, his defenselessness appeared; he had entered the country under a false passport and could be arrested whenever the Department of Justice chose to move. Because he had arrived in San Francisco eighteen months before our declaration of war, he was given the benefit of the doubt. Not until his character as a dangerous enemy alien had been established was he interned. He will be deported at the end of the war.

Different in detail, but similar in character and outcome, was the Odyssey of a missionary of German culture, whose earnings were as nominal as his expenditures were excessive. Arriving in New York in 1912, also by way of the Argentine, he had spent the intervening time travelling about the country in various rôles which would bring him in contact with rich Americans of German birth or blood. At various times he was a dealer in pictures, in stocks and bonds, and in subscription editions of the German classics.

As a side line, he seems to have been checking up American efforts to develop sources of potash, Germany's one great monopoly in minerals. He even engaged himself as stock salesman for an Eastern company organized to extract potash from the Pacific kelp fields and made at least one trip to the coast to study that new industry. Always his scale of living was far in excess of his earnings from such sources of income as could be traced. After a long and patient inquiry—covering nearly eight months from the time the man's pro-German utterances were first reported—he was finally interned for the duration of the war.

Enemy aliens have not been alone in keeping League members up at night. Far more numerous have been the investigations bearing upon the character and loyalty of American citizens, particularly candidates for commissions in the Army and Navy and applicants for civilian service in positions of trust. Still a third class of inquiries which have lacked the thrill of espionage cases have been the thousands of investigations made of claims for exemption or deferred classification under the selective service law.

Anything like a divided allegiance, of course, would destroy the usefulness of an army or naval officer—if, indeed, it did not make him a positive menace to his country. Every character and loyalty inquiry, therefore, has this background of danger, especially when the subject is of German or of Austrian ancestry. And sometimes the League operative must have a keen scent for significant minor details to detect the danger signal.

For instance, one of the candidates for a recent special officers' training camp was a young Cincinnati man with a German name. He was a citizen, of draft age, of such intelligence, experience, and physique that his acceptance was a foregone conclusion if his loyalty were assured. Investigation showed him to have been pro-German in his sympathies before our declaration of war, and practically silent on war subjects since. His attitude was correct; and his application for training was a positive count in his favour. But the League investigator, digging around for information, learned that his man had been a contributor to a fund raised by a Gaelic newspaper for the defence of Sir Roger Casement, when that famous Irish rebel was on trial in London.

If the man had been of Irish blood, such a contribution would have had little significance; natural sympathy for a compatriot in trouble might have prompted it. Such an act by a German or an American, however, suggested more than a passing interest in the violent pro-German, anti-English propaganda which this particular weekly exploited. Verifying the story by reference to the files of the newspaper, the investigator called attention to the fact in his report, and gave it as his opinion that the candidate wanted a commission to escape the draft and that he lacked the whole-hearted loyalty and enthusiasm an Army officer must have to be successful. And, as the final decision coincided with the investigator's, the application was refused.

Another incident—double-barrelled in its effect—has also its humorous side. One of the Chicago League officials picked up two deserters on Michigan Avenue early one evening last December. Neither had an overcoat, one had evidently "hocked" his blouse to provide food or drink. The League man knew he must turn them over to the police, but the boys were so cold and wretched that he determined to give them a good dinner before surrendering them.

At his club, his "guests" created a certain amount of stir—and seemed to enjoy it. They "didn't miss a station from soup to cigarettes," as one of them expressed it. They were finishing up when a young man in a captain's uniform came over and interjected himself into the feast.

"Excuse me," he began as the host arose, "may I ask what your interest in these men is?"

His tone was a shade too crisp, even for so young a captain.

"May I ask yours?" the League man countered.

"I'm in command of the provost guard in Chicago," the other declared. "It's my business to look after deserters."

It was a fatal bit of brag. The League man knew the provost marshal—knew this fellow was an imposter. But one job at a time.

"I know these chaps and I'm looking after them," he answered. "Come along, boys." And they departed in the olive splendour of a taxicab. Then it pulled up a little later before a red light, and a policeman opened the door. The lads were crestfallen but game.

"It was bully while it lasted," they declared. "Anyway, they'd have got us sooner or later."

Before noon next day the youthful pseudo-captain was wiping his tears away and explaining why he had been impersonating an officer. There was a group of musical comedy girls in the foreground and a trail of forged checks and unpaid club and hotel bills in the background. He is learning in Leavenworth prison, now, that the lion's skin is dangerous apparel and that discretion is the better part of a masquerade.

The League files are crammed with reports which have blacker themes—or the scarlet motive which stands for constructive treason. There are folders that deal with reported graft in the purchase of materials for Army camps and subsequent fires which covered up the scanting of buildings. There are others on cases of undue influence brought to bear on members of exemption boards; and sickening instances of "quacks" who have ruined strong but cowardly young bodies for blood money. There are tales of extortion by shyster lawyers for filling out questionnaires—and other tales of money paid by enemy aliens to disreputable "fixers" for pretended protection against the draft.

The mere classified index of the master file at Washington intrigues the imagination. Just a glance at the main "guides" will indicate the range:

Enemy aliens
Unfriendly neutrals
"First-paper" aliens
Disloyal citizens
Pro-German "radicals"
Native-born
Naturalized
Disloyal Government employees
Possible spies or German agents
Pro-German applicants for Government positions
Citizens or aliens living in luxury without visible sources of income
Suspicious foreigners
Enemy propaganda
(Twenty sub-heads here)
Enemy alien funds

Alien extortion cases
I. W. W. agitators
Check of jury panels to keep out pro-Germans
Incendiary fires in war-material plants
Wireless stations
Bomb and dynamite cases
Passport applicants
Seditious utterances
Seditious publications
Seditious meetings
Anti-military activities
Organizations to resist draft
Attempted draft evasions
False exemption claims
Physical disability
Dependent relatives
Desertion of wife to enlist in Army
Fraudulent claims of marriage
Army deserters
Impersonation of officers
Sale of liquor to soldiers and sailors
Sale of narcotics to men in service
Hotel surveillance of doubtful transients
Liberty Bond and Red Cross slackers
Theft of Red Cross supplies
Hoarding of foods
Destruction of foods
Character and loyalty of applicants for commissions

In making these investigations the League has coöperated, not only with the Department of Justice, but also with Army Intelligence, Navy Intelligence, the Alien Property Custodian, the Food Administration, the

Shipping Board, the Red Cross, the Y. M. C. A., and with various other offices at Washington.

The number and variety of cases handled have not constituted the major service of the League, however. Rather, it has been the character and intelligence of the membership—the ability to enter and comb any social, professional, or business circle for information without betraying that an inquiry was afoot. From this angle alone the original idea was pretty close to an inspiration, since it improvised in the hour of need such an organization as not even a generation of effort and many million dollars could have built up.

Just because it was improvised and its personnel kept secret, the League could meet the most dangerous German agents on their own ground and paralyze their efforts by keeping them guessing. Propaganda dies on the lips of the man who can't be certain that his listener is not making mental notes for an official report of the conversation. And the most subtle scheme of spying or sabotage is bound to drag when the plot master is harassed by doubts of the native-born or naturalized accomplices he must enlist for its execution.

One instance to show how much a local organization must depend upon its specialists. Last summer it became necessary to know beyond question whether or not a prominent young German-American in a seaboard city was supplying the funds for the local agitation against the draft. Suspicion attached to him because he spent many evenings aboard his fast-racing schooner in the yacht club harbour, and could not be induced, in any polite and casual way, to invite any of the League's yachting members aboard. His crew, two Scandinavians, were as voluble as oysters.

The schooner was being tuned up for the annual club cruise late in July. Two extra sailors would be needed for the race. The League provided one of them. An upstanding young American, too young for the first officers' training camp but in line for the second, was taken into the League, carefully coached, and turned loose in the harbour with a loaned cat-boat to impress the German-American skipper with his sailing skill. The boy finessed his approach successfully and was asked to train with the crew. But he found nothing material to report until the schooner had actually won the big race.

That night after the victory had been celebrated in a flood of champagne, which he alone avoided, he quietly went through all the private papers in the owner's cabin, made notes, or copied all that referred in any way to pro-German activities and returned by rail to the home port next morning. It turned out that the owner had been guilty of no real disloyalty, though he had skirted the edge more than once; but his papers pointed straight to the real source of the propaganda and the latter was speedily apprehended.

Another interesting case was that of a noted pro-German "pacifist" who for months was kept under surveillance without evidence being secured which would bring a conviction under the existing law. He had declared again and again that nine out of ten Americans were opposed to the war; that thousands of armed men in Arizona, New Mexico, and western Texas were only waiting for the signal to rise against the Government; that another thousand in New York City were watching for the same signal and a leader. He even intimated that he had been asked to be that leader. And though the League could account for every hour of his time, knew every citizen and Congressman he had conferred with and most of the folk he had written to, it was December before an indictment could be secured against him.

That this man is still at liberty, on bail, until the courts reach the hearing of his case is only a detail. The compensating facts are that he served the League for some time as a stalking horse for other citizens and aliens of doubtful loyalty—that ultimately the close watch on him cut down his activities—and that under the amended espionage law any one of a hundred things he did or said would land him quickly in a Federal prison.

In the application of the Selective Service Act the League has taken off the shoulders of the Government one of its heaviest and most important tasks. The draft was and is a favoured field of German agents, who have played upon ignorance and prejudice, religious and union labour fears, racial antipathies, and the baser emotions of cupidity and cowardice. They have utilized every device to persuade men to avoid their military obligations to the country. To the League is assigned the task of checking up all claims for exemptions and all failures to appear before exemption boards. This work, especially in the cities, has entailed enormous labour.

Space forbids a complete review of the League, but at least a paragraph may be inserted about its organization, which is a model of simplicity and flexibility. The League creates and is responsible for its own organization in all of its branches. Executive control of the organization is centred in a Board of National Directors operating from National Headquarters at Washington, D. C., in coöperation with the Attorney-General and the officials of the Bureau of Investigation of the Department of Justice, and through the latter with other departments and agencies of the Government.

In each local office the chief is supreme. He investigates his own men, invites them to join, and directs their work. As already stated, there is a double organization of the local field—a classified organization of trades, professions, industries, hotels, large individual establishments, and office buildings; and a Bureau of Investigation whose organization is territorial. Uniform blanks for reports and records are made up after models supplied by national headquarters, and uniform methods of making investigations are adopted. This simple plan allows each local organization to select the types of men that best suit its needs and to adapt itself entirely to local conditions, while maintaining at the same time complete touch and coöperation with other communities, with the national organization, and with the Government.

The success of the League is attested by Attorney-General Thomas W. Gregory himself. In his annual report to the Congress of the United States he said of the League: "It has proved to be invaluable and constitutes a most important auxiliary and reserve force for the Bureau of Investigation.... This organization has been of the greatest possible aid in thousands of cases.... Its work has been performed in a thoroughly commendable manner with a minimum of friction and complaint and with motives of the highest patriotism. It is a self-supporting organization, and it would be difficult to exaggerate the value of its service to the United States Department of Justice."

CHAPTER X
The German-Hindu Conspiracy

The German-Hindu plot to foment revolution in India is an international drama with touches of "Treasure Island" adventure in the South Seas. The characters include Zimmermann, many German agents in the United States (among them Bernstorff), some venal Americans, and a horde of Hindus—some of them ardent fanatics and some plain grafters. The climax produced several executions, one suicide, two cases of insanity, and a murder. The production cost the Germans more than a million dollars, and the net receipts were a deficit. The scenes were laid in Berlin, Constantinople, Switzerland, New York, Washington, Chicago, San Francisco, Socorro Island, Honolulu, Manila, Java, Japan, China, Siam, and India. The last act was laid in a Federal penitentiary.

Writing from San Francisco, on November 4, 1916, Wilhelm von Brincken, the military attaché of the German Consulate, addressed a letter to his father to be "transmitted through the submarine *Deutschland* on its second voyage from the United States." The letter was never delivered; its boastful first paragraph and its later candid text were read only by agents of the United States Government. Von Brincken began:

MY DEAR FATHER: At last an opportunity presents itself to send an uncensored letter to all of you. May the carrier, Germany's pride, have a happy voyage and reach the home shore unscathed.

He then launched into bitter criticism of his treatment at the Consulate, complaining especially of its niggardly support of his work. Then he wrote (the italics are mine):

As you know, *I am the head and organizer of the Hindu Nationalists on the Pacific*. Revolutionary and propaganda work costs money—much money. Berlin knows that and does not economize. *The Consul General* [Franz Bopp] *also is under instructions to support the movement to the best of his ability and to further it financially*. However, there is a shortcoming in this respect. Whenever money is urgently needed and I report to that effect, I invariably meet with the same opposition. In ninety-nine cases out of a hundred, the required amount is refused. As a result, the work suffers, is delayed, good opportunities are missed, and my people—the Hindus—are frequently exposed to danger of their lives. Just how many fell into the hands of the English and were hung, owing to unnecessary lack of funds, is, of course, wholly beyond our calculation. The "old man" evidently dislikes this type of work and, therefore, has no understanding for it. The other day a Hindu was here, who came directly from Switzerland, as messenger from *Mr. Von Wesendonck, of the Foreign Office (who has charge of Hindu matters there)*. This Hindu wondered why work in San Francisco dragged in such a manner and I told him quite frankly that if the Hindu work were not reorganized from the ground up, and made independent of the Consulate, the work would not only suffer but half of it would be harmful.

Later in the letter he says:

My Hindu described Wesendonck as a particularly pleasing and fine person.

These extracts were written in November of 1916. They illuminate an earlier cable from Von Wesendonck's chief, Zimmermann (the German Foreign Minister in Berlin) written in February of 1916 to Bernstorff at Washington, which was "transmitted respectfully for your information" to Von Papen in New York, and which reads as follows:

Berlin, Feb. 4, 1916.

The German Embassy,

Washington.

In future all Indian affairs are to be exclusively handled by the Committee to be formed by Dr. Chakravarty. Dhriendra Sarkar and Heramba Lal Gupta, which latter person has meantime been expelled from

Japan, thus cease to be independent representatives of *the Indian Independence Committee existing here*.

Zimmermann.

In other words, before February, 1916, the German Government had been plotting with Hindus in the United States for the national independence of India. Indeed, they had begun the work before 1914, and they had become active in it in July of that year—before they started the World War, but after they had decided to start it. By December, they were directing Indian plots from Berlin with ramifications in nearly every neutral country in the world. Two of these plots were hatched in the United States—one in San Francisco and one in Chicago. They were conspiracies to organize military expeditions to India. Our Government spoiled both of them, and the day after we went into the war, or on April 7, 1917, the United States' authorities arrested thirty-four German-Hindu plotters in half a dozen cities and subsequently convicted them all but one of conspiracy.

The story begins in San Francisco. In 1911, a fanatical Indian agitator named Har Dayal came to this country. He worked among the large colonies of turbaned Hindu labourers on the Pacific Coast who had succeeded the Chinese and Japanese coolies in the orchards and gardens and on the railroad tracks in that region of abundant climate and scarce labour. Dayal organized the Hindu Pacific Coast Association and established its headquarters in San Francisco, to which these men came looking for a job or a night's lodging, and where they were fed on rice and revolution. Dayal next established a printing plant and began to publish a paper called *Ghadr*, which means *The Revolution*. The *Ghadr* was out for blood. It preached Hindu uprising in terms of assassination and dynamite.

The first number of the *Ghadr* was published in November, 1913. At once it disclosed a German influence. In the issue of November 15, 1913, it printed these sentences: "The Germans have great sympathy with our movement, because they and ourselves have a common enemy (the

English). In the future Germany can draw assistance from us, and they can render us great assistance also."

As the World War approached, this German influence became more manifest. On July 21, 1914, two days before Austria's ultimatum to Serbia, the *Ghadr* said:

"All intelligent people know that Germany is an enemy of England. We also are mortal enemies of England. So the enemy of our enemy is our friend."

A week later, the *Ghadr* welcomed the approach of war:

"If this war does not start to-day, it will to-morrow. So welcome! India has got her chance.... Hasten preparations for meeting with the speed of wind and storm, and no sooner the war starts in Europe, you start a mutiny in India."

And on August 4th it declared:

"O Warriors! The opportunity that you have been searching for years has come ... there is hope that Germany will help you."

In all this the United States had no interest. We were neutral, and what Germany did to England was (we thought) England's lookout. Also, we were "the asylum of the oppressed" and "the home of free speech"—and if the Hindus thought they ought to talk revolution we were not concerned. It was not until the Hindus and the Germans started "gun running" from our West Coast that we took a hand.

Har Dayal, nevertheless, was too ferocious even for the home of free speech. Early in 1914, he made speeches so villainously offensive to common decency and order that he was arrested and held for deportation on the ground of being an undesirable alien. He jumped bail in March and fled—to Berlin. He arrived there about the time the war clouds began to darken the skies of Europe, and found a sympathetic haven in the German Foreign Office. In company with other Hindu revolutionists, and under the fostering care of Von Wesendonck, he organized that "Indian Independence

Committee existing here" of which Zimmermann spoke affectionately in his cable to Bernstorff, already quoted.

In Har Dayal's place in San Francisco arose another Hindu revolutionary leader, one Ram Chandra. He succeeded to the management of the Hindu Pacific Coast Association, to the editorship of the *Ghadr*, and to the sympathetic understanding with the German agents in San Francisco. These German agents were Bopp, the consul-general, and his staff, of whom Von Brincken, the military attaché, was the agent with whom all personal dealings were carried on. Of the scores of Hindus with unpronounceable names and of their noisy speeches and noisome writings, there is no need to make record. But the warlike activities of the Hindus and their German friends were important, dangerous, and interesting.

On January 9, 1915, W. C. Hughes, of 103 Duane Street, New York, shipped ten carloads of freight to San Diego, Cal. The freight bill was heavy—$11,783.74—and it was prepaid by a check on the Guaranty Trust Company, signed by a German named Hans Tauscher. This German was the well-known American agent of Krupps, and it later developed that the ten carloads of freight were eight thousand rifles and four million cartridges. They were sent to "Juan Bernardo Bowen," in care of M. Martinez & Company, ship brokers of San Diego.

This same "Bowen," whose home address was given as Topolobampo, Mexico, acting through the same Martinez & Company, on January 19th, chartered a sailing vessel for a round trip from San Diego to Topolobampo. This vessel was the *Annie Larsen*. The charter price was $19,000, and this money was paid by J. Clyde Hizar, of San Diego, "Bowen's" attorney. Hizar got the money by wire from a bank in San Francisco, which in turn got it from a woman depositor, who in turn got it from Von Brincken, who in turn got it from the German Consulate's funds. This roundabout method was, of course, designed to conceal the German source of the money.

At about the same time, a company was organized in San Francisco to buy the oil tanker *Maverick* from the Standard Oil Company. Fred Jebsen, former lieutenant in the German Navy, put up the money. The *Maverick* was commanded by Captain H. C. Nelson, and her movements were directed by a young American adventurer, J. B. Starr-Hunt, whom Jebson put aboard as super-cargo ("super-cargo" is an agent put aboard ship by the owner of the merchandise to have charge of the cargo). Parts of a statement subsequently made by young Starr-Hunt tell the rest of the story of the *Maverick* and the *Annie Larsen*:

"I was born in San Antonio, Texas, in November, 1892. I went to a German school in Mexico for nine years. Then I was at Dr. Holbrook's school for four years at Ossining-on-Hudson, New York. I was then for a year at the University of Virginia; three months at the University of Pennsylvania at Philadelphia. Besides this I always had private tutors. After leaving the last-named college I joined my father's law office in Mexico City. This was in the latter part of 1912. My father is one of the leading foreign lawyers in Mexico. In December, 1912, I started for San Francisco to join F. Jebsen & Co., a German firm of shipping agents. I worked in Jebsen's office from February, 1913, to April, 1915; that is, up to the time I joined the *Maverick*. I was not actually in Jebsen's office all this time; I made several trips to various parts of the U. S. A. and Mexico.

"About 1st April, 1915, while I was at Chihuahua, I got a telegram from Jebsen asking me to proceed at once to Los Angeles. I met Jebsen there. He asked me if I cared to proceed to San José del Cabo on the *Maverick* and then transfer to another ship, the *Annie Larsen*, either at San José del Cabo or at any other point on the Mexican coast. He told me that the *Annie Larsen's* cargo consisted of war material, which was to be transhipped to the *Maverick* at whatever point they should meet in Mexican or Central American waters; that a man named Page (I do not remember his initials, but perhaps they were A. W.) who would be on the *Annie Larsen*, was to take charge of the *Maverick*, and that I myself was to take over the *Annie Larsen* and proceed to trade with her in whatever manner I might wish to, for six months, between Mexican or Central American ports, but I was not to return to any American port until after the expiration of six months. He did not tell me why the *Annie Larsen* was not to return to an American port for six months, but the reason was quite clear to me. As a matter of fact, I had heard while I was in Chihuahua that the *Annie Larsen* had departed from San Diego with a cargo of war material, presumably for some belligerent faction in Mexico. She had cleared from San Diego for Topolobampo. This fact had given rise to considerable comment and notoriety. American papers had taken the matter up, and the several arrests of Americans and Mexicans made by the Government in San Diego at the time were popularly believed to have been in connection with the *Annie Larsen* and her cargo. Evidently Jebsen, therefore, thought that, if the *Annie Larsen* returned immediately to an American port, complications might arise. Jebsen was not explicit as to either the destination, or the purpose, of the cargo. One thing I was, however, sure of was that it was not intended for the Mexican rebels. All that Jebsen told me was that the cargo was intended for the Orient, and in the course of conversation he once mentioned Borneo.

"On the (?) of April, the *Maverick* finally sailed from Los Angeles. On the morning of that day Jebsen gave me a sealed letter, addressed to nobody, with verbal instructions to hand it over to Page on the *Annie Larsen* immediately after I met him. Jebsen seemed to be anxious regarding this letter, and warned me to be careful and to see that it fell into no other hands. He also handed me another unaddressed letter to be given to the same man. This was an open letter which I read soon after leaving Los Angeles. There were two enclosures which were printed. One was a circular or memorandum of instructions as to how to work the machine gun or a small Hotchkiss, the diagram of which was given on the second enclosure. I am not quite certain of the type of weapon drawn on that second enclosure, but I think it was one of the two I have mentioned. The printed circular was evidently from the makers of that arm, but the manufacturer's name was carefully cut out from it. Jebsen also handed me a third letter, without address, for Page, and open. It contained typewritten instructions as to how to stow the cargo to be transhipped from the *Annie Larsen*. It was just a short note, more in the nature of a suggestion than instructions. It said that the cases containing rifles were to be stowed in one of the two empty tanks of the *Maverick* and flooded with oil. The ammunition cases were to be stowed in the other empty tank, which was not to be flooded except as a last resort. This note, too, was intended for Page. There was a fourth open note for myself which contained suggestions as to what I should do in future with the *Annie Larsen*. Jebsen, at the same time, made over to me a bundle, consisting of about ten letters, with instructions to hand it over to Page. All these letters were addressed to Captain Othmann. Although Jebsen did not tell me so, I concluded that 'Page' and 'Othmann' were one and the same man, and that 'Page' was an assumed name.

"The day before sailing Jebsen introduced me to a man named B. Miller, who, he said, was a Swedish mining engineer, and who was going on the *Maverick* as far as San José del Cabo, to proceed thence to the mines near La Paz. Jebsen asked me to assist Miller in taking five 'Persians' from Los Angeles to San Pedro, and in finding quarters for them there for the night as they were to go on board the *Maverick* the following day. Jebsen told me nothing about these five Persians except that they were going with the *Maverick* as passengers right through to her destination, and were to be signed on the articles as anything. Accordingly I met Miller again the same evening at the Los Angeles railway station. I found five black men with him. On seeing me, he said: 'Here are my men.' He purchased tickets for them, and we all left by train for San Pedro, where I found lodgings for them in a cheap boarding-house for the night.

"The next morning I went on board the *Maverick* at San Pedro, where I met the Port Commissioner and the crew, who were already on board signed on. Captain Nelson was present. Miller signed on as 'store-keeper' and the five Persians as 'waiters.'

"One of the five Persian waiters, named Jehangir, was evidently the leader and generally kept himself away from the rest. As far as I remember, the names of the others were Khan, Dutt, Deen, and Sham Sher. Later on I discovered that all these were false names. Jehangir's real name, I believe, was Hari Singh; he signed his accounts and receipts as Hari Singh. I have no idea of the real names of the others.

"Five days after leaving Los Angeles we arrived at San José del Cabo, 27th April, I think. There Miller left us, and there, at Nelson's instance, I applied for and got fresh clearance for 'Anjer, Java, via Pacific Islands.' This is the first time that any definite port was mentioned to me as the *Maverick's* destination. There were evidently two reasons for not obtaining this clearance from the original port of departure; first, they did not want the American authorities to know the precise destination of the *Maverick*, which already had roused a certain amount of suspicion; and, secondly, because, I am sure, such a clearance as we desired would not be granted by any American port. According to it the *Maverick* could have touched at every island in the Pacific before arriving at Anjer. Jebsen had given me to understand that we might meet the *Annie Larsen* at San José del Cabo, but she was not there; so we left that port on the 28th of April and proceeded to Socorro Island where we arrived at 9 P. M. on the 29th and anchored in a bay some thirty yards off the shore. As we anchored, Nelson informed the crew that he was expecting to meet at that place the schooner *Annie Larsen* and asked them to be on the lookout for her. Altogether we were twenty-nine days at that island waiting for the schooner, which did not turn up after all. By the time we had anchored it was very dark and the first sign of life on the island was as camp fire close to the shore. Shortly after, a small boat pulled alongside with two American sailors in it. One of them came on the bridge and saw the captain, and after putting the question 'Are you the people who are looking for the *Annie Larsen*?' and getting a reply in the affirmative, he said that the *Annie Larsen* had been at the island, and being short of water, had left some thirteen days before. He delivered a note to Nelson stating that it was left by the *Annie Larsen's* super-cargo, Page. Nelson passed the note over to me to read. It was a short note in English, saying: 'This will be delivered to you by a member of the crew of the schooner *Emma*, who will explain his own position. I have been waiting for you a month, and am now going to the Mexican West Coast for supplies and water. I will return as soon as possible. Please await my return.' (Signed) 'Page.'

"The sailor man then told the following story: that he and his companion in the boat and two Mexican customs-house officials, who were in camp ashore, had left San José del Cabo some time before on the small American schooner *Emma*, with a cargo of bark for the Mexican port of Loreto; that the captain had proven himself incompetent, and they had lost their bearings, and after sailing for many days had eventually arrived at this island, which the master declared was a point close to Manzanillo, but which they discovered to be an island. The mate had died at sea; the master's name was Clarke. These four men declined to go any farther with the captain of that ship and preferred to be left on the island on the off chance of being picked up by a passing vessel. The captain and the cook, the only other members of the crew, had left some days earlier for the Mexican coast. At the same time the *Emma* touched the island the *Annie Larsen* was there, and she provided the castaways with three empty water tanks, a rifle, and a few provisions. Since the departure of the *Annie Larsen* they were hoping for assistance being sent to them from the Mexican coast. We subsequently discovered that these castaways had rigged up a sort of condenser with the aid of their tanks and some old piping.

"The castaway who came on the *Maverick* at Socorro further told us that Page had told him that he had left another letter buried somewhere on the island close to the shore by the bay, which could be easily found if we would make a search for it. Assisted by some of the castaways I made a search for the second note left by Page and found it buried in a bottle under a sign which read: 'Look Here.' The second note was a lengthy repetition of the first. Page asked us to help the castaways but cautioned us not to take them aboard our ship. He said he would return as soon as he could get water and that we were to wait for him. I returned to the ship with the note and read it out to Nelson. Disregarding Page's warning not to take the castaways aboard, he immediately asked them to come aboard, if they cared, which they did. They remained on the *Maverick* till the 6th of May when the American collier (Government ship) *Nanshan* arrived and took them off.

"The following Thursday, 13th May, H. M. S. *Kent* arrived; two officers boarded us immediately and examined our papers. They returned and came on again the next morning accompanied by several marines. They made a thorough search of the vessel this time and returned to their ship. Nelson returned the call. On his return Nelson told me that the *Kent's* commander had questioned him rather closely as to what the *Maverick* was doing there and that in reply he had told him that he could not disclose his real purpose but in a roundabout sort of way hinted that she was there in connection with the Mexican troubles. The *Kent* remained there for about forty hours, during which I struck up an acquaintance with several of the officers. I directed them where good fishing and shooting were to be had and provided them with a few supplies. Although there was no water to be had on that island there were plenty of wild sheep. I am unable to say how they existed without water outside the rainy season.

"The *Annie Larsen* not turning up, we left about the 26th of May. Just before we left I went ashore and left there two notes in bottles for the *Annie Larsen* addressed to Page in case the ship should turn up after we had left. I put one of the bottles in a conspicuous place in the castaways' camp. This note read as follows: 'Consult our Post Office.' by 'our Post Office' I meant the place where Page himself had buried his note for us. The other bottle I buried where I had found Page's, and put up another signboard saying 'Look again.' This note told Page all that had occurred during our stay at the island and that we were going somewhere where we could get further instructions.

"Immediately after the first boarding party from H. M. S. *Kent* had left the *Maverick* after going through our papers, I was sent for by Captain Nelson on the bridge. When I got up there I found him in conversation with Jehangir. I gathered from Nelson that Jehangir had aboard two sacks and six suitcases full of literature which he was very anxious to hide from the *Kent*. We were expecting another visit from the *Kent* for the purpose of searching the ship, and Jehangir said he would not like the literature to fall into the hands of the *Kent* party. Jehangir did not like the idea of destroying the literature and suggested that it should be quietly taken ashore and buried there, pending the departure of the *Kent*. Neither Nelson nor myself fell in with the suggestion and were of opinion that it should be destroyed straight away, if it were dangerous to retain it. Jehangir eventually agreed to this and said he would just keep a sample of the various papers and pamphlets he had. Nelson grumbled even at that. I am not sure whether Jehangir did really preserve any specimens, but I think he did. The two sacks with their contents and the contents of the six suitcases were immediately burnt in the engine room. I personally saw some of this literature. It was all printed matter in a character unknown to me. Some of it was in newspaper form, some in leaflets, but most of it was in the form of pamphlets; the outside cover being mostly pink. The six empty suitcases were appropriated by various members of the crew, I took one of them myself, and it is with me at the present moment. Later I learned from Jehangir that the literature was printed in San Francisco and copies of it 'existed' in Constantinople and Berlin.

"After depositing the two notes on the shore, we weighed anchor. Nelson informed me that he intended proceeding to San Diego....

"After about thirty hours' absence ashore at San Diego the party returned to the *Maverick*, bringing with them a few supplies. Nelson informed me that he was now going to Hilo, Hawaii, and when we were well under way he told me that from the Brewster Hotel, San Diego, he had rung up Jebsen at San Francisco on the long distance telephone and was told in reply to wait at the hotel until he heard from him (Jebsen) further. The following morning he got a wire from Jebsen instructing Nelson to proceed to Hilo, Hawaii, where he would receive further orders. Nelson said he had no word of the *Annie Larsen*.

"We left for Coronados Island on or about the 2d of June and arrived at Hilo on or about the 14th. Port officials came alongside and demanded who we were and what our business was. The captain told them what sort of clearance we had and that we had entered Hilo to communicate with his owners. At about 8 P. M., when it was dark, Captain Elbo, of the war-bound German merchantman *Ahlers*, came alongside in a small dinghy rowed by one German sailor and asked to be allowed aboard to speak to the captain.

Nelson spoke to him over the rail, declining to take the German captain aboard as the health officer had not cleared the ship, but offered to see him the following morning. Before Elbo left, however, he passed a note up to Nelson, who showed it to me later on in his cabin. It read as follows: '*Maverick* is to proceed to Johnson Island and then await the arrival of the schooner *Annie Larsen* and the rest of the ship's programme is to be just as settled before,' namely, that after transferring the cargo to the *Maverick*, the *Maverick* was to proceed on her original voyage.

"Later Captain Elbo took us to the office of Hackfield & Company. There we met a young German named Schroeder who, Elbo gave us to understand, was the chief representative of the Maverick Company at Honolulu and had specially come down to Hilo to meet Nelson about *Maverick's* future plans. It appeared that while we were still at the Collector's office a war-telegrams slip had been out, and among other items of interest was mentioned the arrival in Hilo of the mysterious ship *Maverick*, whose captain had made a statement that he had been trading in the South Sea Islands and he intended leaving for Anjer, Java, stopping at Johnson Island on the way. Schroeder had seen this slip just before we called on him and was apparently highly indignant that Nelson should have disclosed the future movements of the *Maverick* to the press representative. Schroeder told Nelson that it would be impossible for him to permit him, Nelson, to go on to Johnson Island after the news had been made public and that he, Schroeder, would have now to recast his plans. He asked Nelson to wait at Hilo till he should hear from him from Honolulu, where he, Schroeder, must return to arrange for fresh plans. At Nelson's request Schroeder authorized Hackfield to pay all bills 'O. K.'d' by Nelson and to give him such money as he might require.

"Thus we were at Hilo close on two weeks, during which time I personally attended to all the ship's needs. I was assisted by Captain Elbo.

"A couple of days before we sailed from Hilo, Nelson and I met Elbo and another captain of a war-bound German merchantman in Honolulu, who, we were told, had specially come down to give Nelson final instructions. The Honolulu captain told us that the original plans of the

Maverick were now finally abandoned, as it was impossible to use the *Maverick* any more for the purpose she was intended for, in view of the notoriety she had obtained. The *Maverick* was now to proceed to Anjer, Java, calling at Johnson Island; that on arrival at Anjer she was to clear for Batavia and report herself to Behn Meyers, the Maverick Company's agents. Elbo and the Honolulu captain came aboard the *Maverick*. The Honolulu captain had a private talk with me alone in my cabin. He handed me a sealed packet which evidently contained a plate of something heavy. The letter was unaddressed. I was instructed to hand this over to Helfferich at Behn Meyers upon arrival in Batavia. I did not know then who this Helfferich was, nor did I ask who he was. I was merely told that he was the manager of Behn Meyers. I was asked to be careful of that letter, and I was not to give it to anybody else. Shortly after, the Honolulu captain and Elbo left, and we put to sea.

"When we were a couple or three days out of Hilo, Hari Singh, during a conversation, referred once more to the literature we had destroyed at Socorro, and said that it was the product of many of his countrymen who were in America and that he himself had contributed to it. He claimed to have the whole of it by heart and could repeat it without mistake. He was evidently an exile, for he said that 'during the many years of his exile from India' he had at various times written a good deal against the British rule in India. He gave me to understand that formerly he belonged to the Indian Army. He said his home was in the far interior of the country inhabited by ignorant classes, and that if he could only succeed in getting to them, he would easily incite them to revolt against the British Government by promising to provide them with arms and ammunition. He was still under the impression that we were on our way to India, and said that he knew the place we were bound for very well, and so did the other four, and that he could be of great assistance after we got there.

"We got to Johnson Island five days after our departure from Hilo. There was no *Annie Larsen* there. I went ashore together with the mate and left a bottle with a message as follows: 'The American steamer *Maverick* entered and cleared here to-day.' We left there the same afternoon and made for

Anjer, Java. After over three weeks' voyage we arrived at Anjer about the 20th of July. After examination we asked for and obtained permission to proceed to Batavia, and we set sail the same afternoon accompanied by a Dutch torpedo boat. Early next morning we arrived outside Batavia, and later we were taken into port by the harbour master.

"Two or three days outside Anjer I read the letter made over to me by Jebsen at Los Angeles for Page. Owing to Jebsen's warning to be careful about it, I had always carried this letter on my person so as not to lose it. The result was that the envelope had almost fallen to bits; now and again I put the letter, together with the old cover, into a new envelope, but toward the end they, too, got broken up. So I had not to open it to read it. The contents were type-written in German, and were a sheet and a half of the ordinary square business paper. As far as I am able to recollect, the letter read as follows: 'Upon the meeting of the *Annie Larsen* with the *Maverick* at ... (blank) the transhipment of the cargo must be commenced at once. The official reason to be given out was that the *Maverick* is going to Batavia or some other Oriental port to be sold or chartered. It may be suggested that she is good for oil trade on the China Coast. The cases containing rifles should be stowed in one of the two empty tanks and flooded, and the cases of ammunition should be placed in the other, but need not be flooded unless as a last resort. *Maverick* should then proceed to Anjer, Java. No attempt is to be made to escape from British warships, if encountered at sea, nor should she try to avoid meeting merchantmen or warships of other nationalities. In case of her meeting a warship she should act in a manner absolutely open and above suspicion. In case of her being boarded by enemy officers all cordiality should be shown to them, and, in fact, an inspection should actually be offered, to put them off their suspicion. Under no condition is the steamer or the cargo to be permitted to fall into their hands. Should the cargo be discovered, and should there be no escape from capture, the Captain is ordered not to hesitate to have recourse to the last resort, namely, to sink the ship. Upon arriving at Anjer the *Maverick* will be met in the Sunda Strait by a small friendly boat which will instruct you regarding further details. Should you not be met at Anjer you are to proceed to Bangkok, where you are to arrive toward dusk. Here you will be met by a German pilot who will give you further instructions; should you not be met here, also, you are to proceed to Karachi. Outside Karachi the *Maverick* is to be met by numerous small friendly fishing craft. The fishing craft, together with the five blacks aboard, will attend to the unloading and landing of the cargo. Two of the blacks should go ashore immediately on arrival and proceed inland to notify your arrival to "the people". The remaining three blacks and the friendly natives will assist in burying the cargo. Should no friendly fishing boats meet you, two of the blacks should go ashore and do the notifying of the people.'

"After the mission was over, that is whether the *Maverick* was successful or not, she was to go to Batavia and report to Behn Meyers & Company. The last instruction in the letter was that all undelivered papers were to be handed over to Behn Meyers. In accordance with this I made over the letter to Helfferich on our arrival.

"After we had been in the harbour (Batavia) for about an hour or so a German came aboard and introduced himself as Kolbe, 2d Officer of the war-bound merchantman *Silesia*. Nelson signed me to leave them alone, which I did. After they had conversed for about twenty minutes, Kolbe, Nelson, and myself went ashore together and motored down to Helfferich's residence at Konigsplein W. 8. On the way we stopped at the American Consulate; Nelson went in alone. While waiting for him outside in the car I had a talk with Kolbe. He knew all about the *Maverick* and her mission. When I told him that I should like to interview the manager of Behn Meyers to deliver the letter given to me by Dinart at Hilo, Kolbe replied that Helfferich, the man we were on our way to, was the manager and I could make the letter over to him. Dinart had not mentioned Helfferich by name at the time of handing the letter to me. He asked me just to deliver it to Behn Meyers. When Nelson joined us again we proceeded to Helfferich's place where I met for the first time the brothers Theodore and Emile Helfferich. Kolbe and I retired to another part of the house while Nelson and the brothers held a conversation for half an hour or so. After Nelson had done, he left with Kolbe, leaving me with the brothers. I spent about an hour with them. I gave Theodore Helfferich Dinart's letter which he opened in my presence. It was a typewritten sheet in code. Helfferich said it would take him some time to decode it. The 'weight' inside the letter I have spoken of was what looked like a thin slab of lead enclosed in another cover. Helfferich opened this cover and on seeing that it was a thin slab, threw it aside without taking the trouble of examining it closely. I have no idea what it was for, but I imagine that in case it had to be suddenly thrown overboard the weight inside the cover would sink the letter at once. I told them all about our trip, and showed them the letters I had brought with me. Helfferich read the letter intended for Page, and remarked that the arrangements made at this end were substantially the same as those indicated in the letter. He said the signals were the same, and password was the same, and the code was the same. Emile spoke up and said that he had waited for the *Maverick* for three weeks in the Sunda Strait. They deeply regretted the failure of the *Maverick* in not bringing the arms and said that their arrangements on this side were excellent and they were only waiting the arrival of the cargo when they could have easily put their whole scheme through. They observed that 'the people' in India were all ready and prepared and had only been waiting for the arms to turn up. They did not discuss their own scheme with me. Theodore Helfferich expressed his disgust at the *Maverick* being thrust upon him and could not understand the object of her being sent to Batavia when she was not carrying the cargo, and when she could have as easily returned to America. It was then arranged that I should take up my lodging in a hotel ashore and in the meantime Helfferich would decipher the code letter. Things were to be left alone until he had read that.

"A couple of days after, I was rung up by Helfferich and I went and saw him at his place in the evening. He had deciphered the letter which had 'originated' from San Francisco. Helfferich said that the letter directed the abandonment of the *Maverick*, which was either to be sold or chartered to anybody or that she could be used for any regular purpose if Helfferich so desired. She was, if not sold, to be retained in this part of the world and on no account to be returned to America."

So fizzled the German-Hindu gun-running expedition to India. The *Maverick* had arrived, with five "Persians" and no guns, at a Dutch port in the Indies—not India. The Hindus and the crew scattered to the winds; Starr-Hunt started to return to Los Angeles but was detained by the British authorities at Singapore, and ultimately appeared in the Federal court-room at San Francisco as the chief witness for the Government in its case against the German consul and his staff, the complacent Americans, and the Hindu conspirators. The *Annie Larsen* wandered up and down the Pacific Coast, and finally put in at Hoquiam, Wash., where she was promptly seized and her cargo of arms and ammunition locked up by the United States Government.

Von Brincken bore bitter testimony to the failure of the *Maverick* expedition, in the course of a "Report Concerning My Activities at the Imperial Consulate in San Francisco, California"—a report written November 10, 1916, and intended for the eyes of the German Foreign Office. He said:

"I complied with that instruction and met Ram Chandra and other leaders of the Hindu Nationalists, and there laid the foundation for the entire Hindu work which has since then been carried out here on the Pacific.... Up to the present date, I have fulfilled this assignment absolutely alone.... Mr. Von Schack has seen Ram Chandra only a few times during the entire period—while Consul-General Bopp saw the man only once. I had nothing to do with the ship-matters in connection with the Hindu affair. Therefore, I am not responsible for the failure of the '*Maverick* Expedition.' I had only planned the point of landing at Karachi. Besides, through messengers, I had prepared the populace of the Punjab for the arrival of the *Maverick*."

At the time of the *Maverick* enterprise, and after its failure, the Germans engineered a half dozen plots with the Hindus, looking toward revolution in India. Von Papen in New York directed a scheme for an incursion into north-western India through Afghanistan. The German Consul-General in Chicago shipped two German officers and two Hindu agitators to the Orient to train Hindu soldiers in upper Siam for an invasion of Burma. Wesendonck sent Har Dayal from Berlin to Constantinople to act as chairman of a committee of Mohammedans who were to incite the Mussulman population of India to revolt. Ram Chandra, at the instigation of Von Brincken, sent Hindu emissaries from San Francisco to organize revolutionary movements among the Indians in Manila, Tokyo, Shanghai—even in Seoul and Peking. Other emissaries, gathering men and money or transmitting messages, worked in Panama, in Switzerland, in the Sinai Peninsula, in Sweden—scarcely a country in the world but was touched by a filament of this spider's web of German intrigue.

And, like gossamer, it all came to airy nothingness. A few dacoities [robberies accompanied by violence], a few vain attempts to suborn loyal native troops in India, were the net results of enormous labours, lengthy journeys, and huge expenditures of money.

By December, 1915, the German Government became impatient of this much ado about nothing. But it did not abandon hope. Zimmermann summoned a little, nervous, excitable Hindu from New York to Berlin. Dr. Chakravarty left America on a false passport, and in February, 1916, was appointed in Berlin to head the Indian intrigues in America. Zimmermann's cable to Bernstorff, quoted in the first part of this article, notified the German authorities here of his appointment. By August, Dr. Chakravarty was in San Francisco, consulting with Ram Chandra and the Germans there.

Chakravarty and Ram Chandra had one thing in common—both knew the value of real-estate. Out of their joint operations in the insubstantial pursuit of Indian liberty, each emerged with some perfectly sound investments in mundane property, paid for with money subtracted from the German gold that passed through their hands for the "freeing of the oppressed." Chakravarty put about forty thousand dollars into New York apartments, and Ram Chandra several thousands into residence and business property in San Francisco.

Ram Chandra's real-estate ventures got him into trouble. They gave the needed opportunity to his rival for control of the Hindu organization in California. This rival was Bhagwan Singh, the poet and orator of the

"Movement." Late in 1916, he accused Ram Chandra of stealing Hindu funds. The directors of the Hindu Pacific Coast Association investigated the charge, and threw Ram Chandra out. Bhagwan Singh became president of the association and editor of the *Ghadr*. A few months later, when the United States entered the war, the whole crew was arrested, along with the German agents in San Francisco and Honolulu and with the Americans and German-Americans implicated in the *Maverick* enterprise.

The trial of these men was one of the most picturesque scenes ever enacted in an American court. In the prisoner's dock aggressive blond German officers sat beside anaemic, swarthy, turbaned Hindus and plain American business men. To make the evidence intelligible to the jury, a map of half the world was painted on one wall of the court-room, showing America and Asia and the Pacific Ocean, splotched with red dots and routes of travel. Beside the map were printed the names of the defendants, so that their strangeness might be somewhat simplified. Among the polyglot evidence were Hindu publications in six Oriental languages, including Persian; cipher messages which, when deciphered, proved to be an Indian revolutionist's letters which had to be translated by reference to page and line of an American's book about "Germany and the Germans"; enciphered code, written in Berlin by the German Foreign Minister, transmitted to Stockholm and thence by the Swedish Government to Buenos Aires and thence by Count Luxburg to Bernstorff in Washington, telling him to pay an East Indian in New York money for use in San Francisco to send arms to revolutionists near Calcutta—besides other oddities of men and places and documents too numerous to mention.

The episode of the *Maverick* and the *Annie Larsen* occupied a large place in the trial. One of the humours of that fiasco was the proof that "Juan Bernardo Bowen," of Topolobampo, Mexico, was a romantic imagining to conceal plain Bernard Manning of San Diego. There was no Juan Bernardo. The man who got Tauscher's shipment of arms for the *Annie Larsen* was Manning.

The prosecution proved that the funds for the purchase of the *Maverick* and for the charter of the *Annie Larsen* were got from the German

Consulate's bank accounts in San Francisco, and were concealed by an elaborate jugglery through a chain of American lawyers and shipping agents in San Francisco, Los Angeles, and San Diego.

The end of the story is briefly told in the following despatch to the New York *Sun*, dated San Francisco, April 24, 1918:

Twenty-nine men, charged with conspiring on American soil to start a revolution against British rule in India, were found guilty by a jury in Federal Court early to-day.

Just as court adjourned for the noon recess yesterday, the last day of the trial, Ram Singh, a defendant, shot and killed Ram Chandra, another defendant. United States Marshal James Holohan shot Ram Singh dead in his tracks.

CHAPTER XI
Dr. Scheele, Chemical Spy

One day the Department of Justice in Washington received a brief code message, dated from Havana, saying that "Dr. Scheele" was coming home. The War Department also had received a code message; these started a little hum of activity. The messages gave a key to the possession of certain papers. Hurriedly a special agent of the Department of Justice was provided with a letter written in the cipher designated. The agent spoke German, looked German, and hastened to the home of an unsuspecting custodian of some of the Fatherland's most damaging records, and there arranged with the guardian for a safer place for such papers. But the duly-accredited messenger wasn't German at all, and the papers handed over widened out the trail of one big German plot.

Who was this Dr. Scheele? He was a quiet German chemist who sometimes aided the police in detecting traces of crime. Didn't his neighbours know him? Of course; he was that genial and entertaining German-American who owned a drug store in Brooklyn, one of the desirable kind of citizens, the law-abiding kind of foreigner whom we welcomed in our midst. Did the business world know him? Yes; he was president of the New Jersey Agricultural Chemical Company, a concern which kept its contracts and paid its debts. America was satisfied with this president, the adopted son, who had married an American wife and resided peacefully among us for twenty-four years. Why not?

When the French liner *La Lorraine* caught fire at sea with hospital nurses and supplies of mercy on board, what could this have to do with an inconspicuous druggist in Brooklyn?—or when numerous ships sailed loaded with sugar or supplies for the needy neutrals abroad, and never after were heard of?

Finally a British cruiser with an inquisitive captain overhauled the steamship *Rize* which was carrying a cargo of fertilizer badly needed for the fields in Denmark. There was nothing particularly suspicious about a cargo packed in sacks, just ordinary brown powdered fertilizer of the most common variety and shipped by the New Jersey Agricultural Chemical Co.

But for some reason the papers didn't entirely satisfy. The cargo was confiscated, analyzed, and an astonished chemist reported that the "fertilizer" was composed of highest grade lubricating oil, mixed with a certain chemical which had reduced the oil to a solid but when the mixture was treated with a little acid the sacks yielded oil fit for the Kaiser's best *Unterseeboten.*

The Department of Justice paid an official call on the New Jersey company—the "President" was away; he remained away during two years of very painstaking search by the officials of the Department's secret service, which had an ever-increasing desire to make the acquaintance of the inconspicuous chemist who seemed to possess some of the mythical powers of the ancient alchemists.

There seemed also to be an unusual bank account connected with this gentleman, engaged in such magnificent business enterprises, that yielded such meagre profits, as were evidenced by the President's home life and general circumstances. Who is he, and where is he? were questions that vexed the bureau in Washington. Two years rolled by; numbers of Germans connected with "the Doctor" were sent to jail, but only rumours were got of trails of the chemist.

Fate, however, transferred our story to the shadowy neighbourhood of Morro Castle; there, an excited and still unidentified German who was trying to board a vessel at Matanzas, Cuba, for a port in Mexico, was brought into Havana in front of the bayonets of a not-too-careful Rural Guard. Then a newly arrived representative of the Department of Justice undertook some negotiations with the Cuban Government for a safe passage back for a certain Dr. Walter T. Scheele and his paymaster.

An ancient fort, which is the military prison in Havana and a part of the old fortified wall which follows the water front of the picturesque harbour, was shrouded in darkness when the hour of departure arrived. Between the old fort and the grim outline of "the Morro" lay a Cuban gunboat with black smoke pouring out of her funnels; a tropical storm blowing in over the Gulf Stream alternately darkened the sky a deeper tone and lit it up with vivid lightning flashes. Presently a little group appeared on the sea walls and a flash of lightning showed an American in plain clothes, the regalia of the agents of Justice and a colonel of the regular army who were signing a receipt for two quiet figures in alpine hats. A courteous Cuban officer saluted and shook hands with the departing guests, handcuffs were silently slipped on to thick German wrists, and the little steam pinnace of the warship sped off through the darkness alongside its gangway.

An interview none the less sombre and creepy occurred on the other side of the Gulf Stream within the walls of Fort Taylor. Two automobiles had driven up in the darkness to an emplacement beneath the shadow of a heavy gun. The party which had left Havana descended in a dimly lighted courtyard where a squad of non-commissioned officers was waiting. One figure in an alpine hat had to be lifted from the automobile while the other stood erect.

Here is the story of Dr. Scheele, the more important of these two agents of the Kaiser:

Twenty-five years ago a German youth (one of the favourite pupils of the great chemist, Professor Keukle) graduated at Bonn. He came of an illustrious family; his grandfather, the Swedish professor, Scheele, discovered chlorine gas. His father, born in Germany, died in the discovery of "prussic acid," the most quickly fatal drug known. The youth, with sixteen deep scars on his head and face from duelling under the vicious German code, was a man of proved valour. Who was better to send to the great developing home of liberty and freedom and study its industry, and prepare for a day which was already dazzling the newly enthroned Kaiser?

Dr. Hugo Schweitzer was chosen to go with him and collaborate. He, as the head of the Bayer Chemical Company—a German concern that practically monopolized the trade in synthetic drugs in the United States—was to report on, to model, or undermine our development of industrial chemistry. Dr. Scheele was to report on and develop the plan and chemistry of warfare, explosives, incendiaries, poison gas, and the products Germany should import and accumulate to make her sure and independent on the day she should strike the world. Did these young men faithfully accomplish their tasks?

Dye making was almost an unknown art in America when the war broke out; chlorine gas was a laboratory curiosity; potash was a German salt—we had been led to believe our millions of tons of the mineral were insoluble. Where necessary, those of our chemists who had learned the secrets were retained and paid. The list of our chemical houses reads like the telephone directory of Unter den Linden, and the Alien Property Custodian has since spent many nights over their affairs.

While the German plenipotentiaries were busy at The Hague agreeing to the elimination of poison gas and incendiaries from warfare, their chemists in the United States, paid regularly but meagerly through the Embassy at Washington, exchanged views in writing and by cable with the chemists of the Fatherland over the most fatal methods for the use of the gas which had just been developed for the purpose.

Mustard gas was used against the Allies in 1917, a new and atrocious device, "only discovered and recently used by the Germans because of the brutality of their enemies." A few formulæ for this product were in Dr. Scheele's laboratory in New York about five years before the war, and tactics of the uses discussed in the trips which he made home every two years "to keep up to date."

Two methods of stifling American production have not yet been mentioned. The first was this: When a man began to make a reputation as a chemist in an American-owned concern, he was hired away to work for a German-owned factory. Salary was no consideration; they simply bid the price required to get him. The second method was: when an American chemist invented a new product or a new process, and patented it, it was bought from him before it could be commercially developed. Again price was no consideration. The only instructions were: "Pay as little as you can, but get it."

The operation of this system was the duty of Dr. Scheele and Dr. Schweitzer. Reporting to them was at least one loyal German chemist in every chemical factory in the United States; dozens of them in the larger ones. At their disposal were the resources of the Imperial German Government. These, too, were made accessible through Dr. Heinrich Albert in German-American banking and brokerage concerns, chiefly G. Amsinck & Company, the Trans-Atlantic Trust Company, and Knauth, Nochode & Kuhne, of New York, every one of them in reality a local American agency of one or another of the imperially controlled banks of Germany and Austria—such as the Reichsbank, the Disconto Gesellschaft, or the Deutsche Bank.

The chief of these American branches was G. Amsinck & Company, operating as commission merchants and private bankers. The head of this concern was Adolf Pavenstedt, an accomplished man of the world, a shrewd banker, and under the iron discipline of the Kaiser's military organization. Pavenstedt lived at the German Club in Central Park South, in New York, took his vacations in Cuba in the winter and the Berkshires in the summer, was received in the best society in New York, passed easily in Wall Street as a man of large personal fortune and of sound business judgment—altogether a characteristic German hypocrite and government agent acting under Dr. Albert and Bernstorff. He was a paymaster of Germany's nation-wide organization to control our industrial life, to spy out our military plans, and to keep us powerless against the day when Prussia should be ready to sweep the world. He was also the financial go-between in the Bolo Pasha case. Fortunately, he has now long been a resident of an Army internment camp.

Two years ago the Government indicted Dr. Scheele for his part in the incendiary bomb plot. The details of this fiendish device will be given later in the story. Dr. Scheele was forewarned of probable detection on the 31st of March, 1916, by a special-delivery letter telling him to see Wolf von Igel immediately at 60 Wall Street in New York. Von Igel told him to start for Cuba by the next train. Dr. Scheele feared that such a precipitate flight would expose him to certain arrest. Hence, he violated his instruction and went south to Jacksonville by easy stages. There he called upon one Sperber, the editor of the Florida *Deutsche Staatszeitung*, who warned him not to sail from Key West, as that port was being watched both by our officers and by the British cruisers outside the three-mile limit. Sperber gave Dr. Scheele letters of introduction and credentials under the name of W. T. Rheinfelder, to act as a correspondent for his paper. He supplied him also with fake calling cards and other forged documents, establishing him in his rôle. Still fearing to leave for Cuba, he waited.

His superiors again instructed him to go to Cuba. He landed in Cuba on April 16th. There he reported to the German Minister, Count Verdy du Vernois, who passed him on to an attaché of the Legation with this strange result: that Dr. Scheele next found himself installed as a "guest" in the house of one Juan Pozas, under the name of James G. Williams, and in the character of a visiting American.

His strange and unexpected host appeared at first to be simply a wealthy Cuban merchant. His manner of life strengthened this impression. Dr. Scheele found himself comfortably installed in a large room in a magnificent house, surrounded by grounds of a city block square, in the suburb Guana Bacca of Havana. In reality, Pozas was the king of the Cuban smugglers. His splendid establishment and his social prestige rested upon a picturesque foundation of the work of silent men in little boats working in the dark of the moon along the tropical Cuban shore.

To Dr. Scheele, Pozas soon appeared to be not only host but jailer. Though he was treated with every courtesy and as a member of the family, he was not allowed outside the house for six months after his arrival. The confinement so told upon his health that he was finally permitted the freedom of the garden, and, to while away the time, he worked among the flowers, making at length a beauty spot of the whole place. At the same time, he was devoting other spare hours to covering the walls of the Pozas mansion with beautiful mural paintings. Again it may be noted that Dr. Scheele is a remarkable man.

In this strange retreat the doctor spent two years. Then suddenly, without warning, he was hurried hither and yon about the island, travelling under guard by automobile by night, and lying hidden by day in the houses of trusted German agents. He finally arrived at Mantanzas. Here, the man in whose house he was to stay hidden became fearful that he would be discovered there and the man himself get into desperate trouble. He, therefore, directed Dr. Scheele to a neighbouring hotel, but the doctor was unable to obtain accommodation, so that he spent the night sitting in a railroad station.

Simultaneously another German of Havana was taken into custody. He was implicated in the Scheele affair by reason of his payments to the doctor, besides being involved in numerous violations of the neutrality of Cuba, for which the Cuban Government meant to hold him responsible.

The close investigation of this man revealed much valuable data. A collection of papers had been buried by Dr. Scheele in the tropical garden he had built about the Pozas mansion. There they were unearthed by the agent of the Department of Justice of the United States who had gone to Cuba to bring him back. Taking a pick and shovel and digging among the flowers cherished by the doctor, he found these damning documents from Potsdam, containing their secret instructions for the working out of the industrial conquest of *Vereinigten Staaten*—These United States.

Another set of documents was obtained by a very clever piece of work by agents of the Department of Justice. These were papers left behind by Wolf von Igel when he left the United States—papers that he dared not risk having seized and read by the British authorities on his way to Germany. They were packed in a suitcase and were committed to the care of a German in Englewood, New Jersey. On instructions from the head office of the Department of Justice in Washington, agents in the New York office of the Department wrote out in German, on a typewriter, the letter telling this German to deliver the suitcase to the bearer and including in its message the magic password. This letter was entrusted to an agent who spoke German perfectly.

He executed the commission without a hitch. He called upon the German and introduced himself in low tones as a loyal subject of the Kaiser and asked to be taken into the house. There he presented his letter. When the German read it, he broke into a hearty laugh and said the password no longer really applied, because it referred to the coal pile. He had found, on account of the coal shortage, that at times he could not keep enough coal in the cellar to keep the suitcase covered, and that consequently he had had to conceal it elsewhere in the house. The caller joined him in laughter at this piece of humour, and the German excused himself and soon returned with the suitcase. It was not till several days later that he had the slightest inkling that the man he had entertained was an operative of the American Government.

The plot for which Dr. Scheele was brought to earth was only a detail in the vast scheme of Germany's treachery, but it was one of the most dastardly and most dramatic of those details, and its detection and unravelling revealed the men at the head of the German system in this country and their mutual relationships. In a previous chapter I have told something of the career of Franz von Rintelen. At this point he appears as an agent of Germany seeking to destroy the ships bearing American supplies to the Allies. One day Dr. Scheele received a caller, Eno Bode, a captain in the service of the North German Lloyd Steamship Company. Bode bore a card from Von Papen, ordering Scheele to execute any orders which Bode gave. Von Papen's orders, in their turn, had come through Rintelen.

Bode now disclosed to Dr. Scheele a most infernal plan. He was instructed to invent a bomb of simple mechanism, which could be placed in a ship's cargo or its coal and which would not explode, but set fire to anything inflammable with which it came in contact. It must be devised to operate at any predetermined time after it was placed on board.

To Dr. Scheele, a great chemist himself and possessed of every secret of the greatest nation of chemists in the world, this was a simple order. In his instructions he was forbidden to apply for his materials to any American concern through which the purchase might ever be traced. Consequently, he asked for technical assistance and was referred to Captain Carl Schmidt, the chief engineer of the *Friedrich der Grosse*, one of the great German liners interned at Hoboken. Schmidt placed at his disposal Charles Becker, the electrician of the *Friedrich der Grosse*. From him he obtained sections of lead pipe and thin sheets of lead and tin. The chemicals were easily obtained from strictly German sources.

Dr. Scheele now made a few experiments and quickly evolved a bomb that was as simple as it was efficient. It consisted merely of a section of lead pipe, about two and a half inches in diameter and three or four inches long. This cylinder was separated into two water-tight compartments by a thin disk of the sheet tin. In one of the two compartments was placed a chemical, and in the other a corrosive acid. The ends were then sealed and the bomb was complete. The acid slowly ate its way through the tin partition, and when at length a tiny hole was made, the acid and the chemical mingled and their action was to produce, without noise, a heat so intense that it melted the lead in the cylinder and the whole bomb flowed down into a molten mass so fervent that it would ignite any ordinary substance, such as coal or wood. No timing mechanism was necessary. The thickness of the tin partition determined the time at which the bomb would act. By careful experiment, Dr. Scheele was able to manufacture bombs that would become effective in two days, four days, six days, eight days—at will. For example, if the tin partition was made one sixtieth of an inch in thickness, the bomb would operate in forty-eight hours. The thickness necessary for the longer periods was established by actual test.

As soon as the bomb was perfected, its manufacture was undertaken on a big scale. Soon the workroom aboard the *Friedrich der Grosse* was turning out thirty-five of these "cigars," as the Germans called them, every day. Altogether, before the game became too dangerous and Dr. Scheele was forced to flee, nearly five hundred bombs were manufactured.

Next came the necessity for an organization to place these bombs upon the ships. First, the ships themselves must be known—their sailing dates, their names, their berths and cargoes. Through German sources of information, the data about merchant ships were gathered and by Dr. Carl

Schimmel, another German agent in New York City, were listed and classified. These records were placed at the disposal of the bomb-placing squad.

Captain Carl Wolpert was in charge of this work. He was the superintendent of the Atlas Line, a subsidiary of the Hamburg-American Steamship Company, and an officer of the German Naval Reserve. Armed by Scheele with the "cigars," by Schimmel with the list of ships, and by Von Rintelen with unlimited money, Wolpert chose a group of trusted lieutenants from among the Germans in New York. These men frequented the water-front and the neighbouring saloons, where they sought out stevedores, who could be bribed to place the bombs where they were directed. Fortunately for the lives of seamen and for the property of the Allies, many of these men took the German money but threw the bombs into the bay. Enough, however, earned their blood money so that many ships were set afire on their voyage across the Atlantic, some of them burning to the water's edge, most of them being greatly damaged, the total loss figuring well up in the millions of dollars. Many a captain in mid-ocean fought the flames on his vessel, from the second or third day of his voyage, all the way into port. A fire would break out in his bunker coal; it might be quenched, only to break out in the cargo two days later, and perhaps a day after that start up again in the coal.

This fiendish work was done in cold blood, do not forget, at the command of the Imperial German Government, at its expense, under the direction of one of its most highly placed aristocrats, by one of Germany's greatest chemists, with the coöperation of officers of the German Navy and with the cognizance of the German Ambassador to our friendly Government. Here was no passion of battle, no extemporized savagery of revenge. It was a calculated atrocity, perpetrated by the highest authorities of one of the most "civilized" of the "Christian" nations, using the most technical processes of one of the most complex arts of modern life. The magic by which the slimy refuse of burning coal is transmuted into dyes which give to paints and fabrics the splendour of the dawn and the beauty of the rose, was here debased to the infamous uses of treachery and murder.

THE END

www.ingramcontent.com/pod-product-compliance
Lightning Source LLC
Chambersburg PA
CBHW061213210726
48294CB00006B/1828

* 9 7 8 1 7 7 4 8 1 8 3 1 2 *